RUNNING THROUGH LIFE

RUNNING THROUGH LIFE

REFLECTIONS FROM 26.2 MILES

TOMMY BRESSON

W. WinePressPublishing
Great Books, Defined.

© 2013 by Tommy Bresson. All rights reserved.

WinePress Publishing (PO Box 428, Enumclaw, WA 98022) functions only as book publisher. As such, the ultimate design, content, editorial accuracy, and views expressed or implied in this work are those of the author.

No part of this publication may be reproduced, stored in a retrieval system, or transmitted in any way by any means—electronic, mechanical, photocopy, recording, or otherwise—without the prior permission of the copyright holder, except as provided by USA copyright law.

The author of this book has waived a portion of the publisher's recommended professional editing services. As such, any related errors found in this finished product are not the publisher's responsibility.

Unless otherwise noted, all Scriptures are taken from the *Holy Bible, New International Version®, NIV®*. Copyright © 1973, 1978, 1984 by Biblica, Inc.™ Used by permission of Zondervan. All rights reserved worldwide. www.zondervan.com

ISBN 13: 978-1-4141-2401-8
ISBN 10: 1-4141-2401-5
Library of Congress Catalog Card Number: 2012910902

DEDICATION

I WOULD LIKE to dedicate this book to my immediate family. Thank you for all of your encouragement, nourishment, support, and love. I am who I am because of you. I love you all more than words can express.

Dad, thank you for taking me on that very first Reggie White run. Your laughter, wisdom, and encouragement have been invaluable.

Mom, thank you for all of the words of encouragement along the way. You always challenge me and help me to see people as Jesus sees them.

Philip, everybody wants an older brother like you. Thank you for your continued support. One of these days I will finally beat you at something!

Whitney, you are beautiful beyond words. Your strength, determination, and perseverance are unparalleled. Never stop making people laugh. Your bubbly attitude changes lives.

DAD

And we know that in all things God works for the good of those who love him, who have been called according to his purpose.
—Romans 8:28

God's Word tells us that he loves us regardless of what circumstances we are going through. While that may be easy to say during an "easy" season of life, it can be a very difficult thing to say while going through a "difficult" season. Dad, I have heard you testify that God is good, all the time. And all the time, God is good. It does not matter what kind of season you are going through, your heart believes that God will work for the good of those who love him.

Dad, I always place a picture of us in this specific spot because it reminds me of the season of your cancer. I look back at those days with mixed emotions. In one sense absolutely no part of me ever wants to revisit those days. To this day, the scent of a hospital brings back a flood of emotions, all taking me back to Portsmouth Hospital and its cancer ward. I can vividly recall your first session of chemotherapy. I can remember when you traveled to my basketball game. I can remember seeing you physically weak. Those days were marked by fear, uncertainty, pain, and worry.

Yet at the same time, those days were monumental in my journey of faith. I remember going to bed not knowing whether or not I would wake up the next morning and see you. The reality of that trial forced me to think about death, and what happens to us after we leave this earth. With that on my mind we found ourselves going to Sunday night praise and worship services, and I stood next to you, seeing you lift up your hands and with tears in your eyes sing, "It is well with my soul." Through those days, and your example, I realized my strength could not come from me. I recognized my hope could not be rooted in anything of this world, rather it had to come from Jesus. As a result of those dark days, and tear-filled nights, I found Jesus as my personal Lord and

Savior. In all things, including cancer, God can work for the good of those who love him.

Therefore, I look back at those days with mixed emotions. They were by no means easy, but I gained something that will never perish. So I often find myself saying, "If I had to go back and do it all again, in order to come out the way I did, I would do it in a heartbeat." Here is the crazy thing … I fully believe that if you were given the opportunity to go back in time and choose whether or not you wanted to go through that trial again, you love me so much that you would go through it all again with joy. That is such an amazing feeling and a beautiful image of a father's love, a love that reminds me of our heavenly Father's love for us.

Beyond that, you have taught me too much to write in one letter. You have always been a man of God whom I have admired and looked up to. You have continually encouraged me and inspired me to be a better man, and to do everything I can to the best of my ability. Your dedication and input to the pages of this book have been monumental. I do not think I could have finished it without your help and encouragement.

Of course, I cannot write without at least mentioning your humor. Your one-liners are priceless and perfectly timed. You can even use the same jokes over and over, and yet every time I still laugh. Your humor is perfectly timed, as it has given refreshment in times of stress and heartache. Don't worry, I won't act like I'm not impressed.

Additionally we have seen some pretty cool things together, and I am always blessed by the time we get to spend together. I love all the different ways we can finish the sentence, "remember that time we …" … saw Kirk Franklin in concert, … saw those soccer games in California, … went to the playoff game at Lambeau Field, … walked the footsteps of the Reformation leaders in Geneva. We have done some pretty incredible things, and while I enjoyed what we were doing, I was even more thrilled to be doing it with you by my side.

Thank you for being a role model. Thank you for all of your wisdom, humor, and love. Thank you for not always giving me what

I want, but always giving me what I needed. Thank you for cheering me on, and inspiring me. Thank you for always encouraging me to be the hardest worker, and to always give my all. Thank you for the perseverance you have shown and instilled in me. Thank you for taking me on all those Reggie White runs. I love you.

MOM

Go, gather together all the Jews who are in Susa, and fast for me. Do not eat or drink for three days, night or day. I and my attendants will fast as you do. When this is done, I will go to the king, even though it is against the law. And if I perish, I perish.
—Esther 4:16

Strength. Determination. Beauty. Conviction. Elegance. When I look at the characteristics of Esther, these are some of the first words that come to my mind. I am blessed because I read about them in the Bible, and I see them lived out in you. You are a living model to me of a woman of Esther's elegance and strength. You are beautiful, not only on the outside, but more importantly, and more impressively, on the inside. I am blessed and privileged to call you my mother.

Your words have always been covered with grace and elegance. As I was growing up, you always had the right words to say. However, it was not the words that really mattered, but the heart behind the words that made the difference. Your heart was always seeking the best for us. Sometimes that meant giving us what we wanted, and sometimes that meant giving us what we needed. Your words are full of compassion, support, and love. I love being on the receiving end of your words, but I also enjoy being a witness to the power of your words. The way in which you encourage, support, and cheer on Dad has always been inspiring. Whatever he does, you believe in him, and your words (and actions) show that.

Your strength is unlike anybody else's I have ever met. To be honest, I don't know how you do it. When I look back at the storms that hit our family year after year upon first moving to New Hampshire, you were strong and determined. The way in which you stood by Dad's side as he fought through his illness is forever engraved in my mind. Whenever he needed to lean on you—physically, mentally, emotionally, or spiritually—you were there for him. And as those storms hit, they knocked you to your knees and you leaned on the everlasting arms of God. Your strength, determination, and love were rooted in Jesus, and because of that they were able to overflow into every room of our house. Our family survived those storms because of your strength and determination, both of which find their foundation in Jesus Christ.

Your inner beauty is truly amazing. You truly have a heart that desires for no person to be alone, for nobody to feel unwanted or unloved. God has placed within you a unique characteristic that searches for the lonely and pulls them in. With this gift you have truly been a blessing to others, and you have done a great job of encouraging me to do the same. You have always reminded me about what it is like to be the new kid and how daunting that can be. Therefore, it has become a natural part of my personality to seek out those who are new and to do my best to make them feel wanted and included. You have also always taught me to see the best in people, and to be a friend to everyone. With this in mind, you have encouraged me to be a friend to those in need of a friend. At certain times in my life I have taken a look at my friends and thought, "How did we become friends?" More often than not I feel the answer lies in the fact that you raised me to see the best in people, and to take the time to get to know them. By doing so, I have formed some lifelong friendships.

In recent years I have continually been blessed by our kindred spirits in ministry. I love how the ministry you are doing in your school mirrors what I am doing in mine. Professionally, we have become peers and it is a blessing to be able to bounce ideas off of you, to pester you with questions, and to gather input on how to handle a certain situation. The numerous walks we embark on discussing school policies, school activities, and discipleship tools have sharpened me.

Mom, thank you. Thank you for all you have done and continue to do in my life. Thank you for your love and friendship. Thank you for all the laughter, all the conversations, and all the encouragement. Thank you for listening when I called home discouraged, hurt, frustrated. Thank you for everything. I love you.

PHILIP

He says, "Be still, and know that I am God; I will be exalted among the nations, I will be exalted in all the earth." The Lord Almighty is with us; the god of Jacob is our fortress.
—Psalm 46:10

There is one specific story in my mind for the reason behind keeping a picture of us tucked away in this precise Psalm. To be honest, I don't know exactly when the story took place, or all the specifics, but I will share what I remember. I've never talked to you about it so I'm not sure if you remember it or not. Regardless, I know it happened, and it will be a memory that will always stay with me.

We were living in Wisconsin at the time, and you and I were riding the bus home from school. As had happened numerous times, my mouth somehow got me in trouble. I thought I was funny; others did not. The bullies who took offense at my words were no longer content sitting multiple seats away; they wanted to get closer to me and pick a fight. At the moment of my ill-timed comment, I was sitting alone. There was one empty seat next to me, and you were across the aisle. After my comments, the bullies came and sat two seats away from me. Then they moved one seat away from me. As they did, you moved across the aisle and sat right next to me. Your presence scared them, so they moved back to two seats away. Two seats away was a safe distance for my safety, so you then moved back across the aisle. Thinking they had a chance to get me, the bullies once again moved one seat away from me. Upon seeing this, you immediately moved back across the aisle, again sitting next to me. This game of cat and mouse happened a few times until the bullies tried to reason with you (perhaps this is where your lawyer skills started), yet you would not give in. This went on for some time, until we finally reached our stop, where we got off the bus. I exited the bus unharmed. You stood up for me and protected me. Every time they moved closer to harm me, you sat right next to me, and would not allow them to touch me.

Perhaps it seems insignificant and maybe it sounds childish to hold onto this memory. But this story is a great reminder that you always have been, and always will be, there for me. The Psalm says to "be still and know that I am God." The psalmist is encouraging us to take a deep breath and recognize that God is on our side. With this knowledge no problem is too big to overcome. This memory of mine continually helps me to be still and remember that I have an older brother.

What does having an older brother mean to me? It means that I always have someone I can look up to. Somebody who I try to emulate and aspire to be like. It means I have someone whom I can call at any point with whatever is on my mind. Whether I need a listening ear, advice, guidance, or the latest news about a sports team, I can call you with whatever is on my heart. I feel as though any situation I face, you have experience with and can give me good, practical, sound advice. Your advice and our conversations commonly remind me of Dad, and his mannerisms. I may send you a three-page email where I am processing through something and attempting to look at it from every angle imaginable. After reading my mini-novel, you respond with a few sentences of advice that leave me satisfied and encouraged.

Having an older brother also means a lot of competition. I believe I am a better competitor and a better person as a result of all our competition. Whether it was basketball in our garage, Mario Kart, or golf, I have always enjoyed our spirit of competition. Being the younger brother I have succumbed to the "younger brother theory," which means no matter what we compete in, I will always lose. One of these days it will move from being a theory to a fact. Regardless, you have pushed me in many ways to become better. And you continually presented opportunities for me to better my humility in defeat.

I cannot finish without one final story. The years we spent on the soccer field together were the most enjoyable and meaningful to me in all my playing career. I remember sitting on the sideline in Manchester next to you as you finished your high school career and you said, "This isn't the way it was supposed to end for us."

Little did we know at the time, but four years later we would once again find ourselves on the sideline of a soccer field after setting numerous collegiate records together. Sitting there you referenced back to the sideline in Manchester and said, "This is more what I imagined."

You did not have a choice as to whether or not you would be my older brother. You did have a choice in what you would do with that role. Thank you for going above and beyond what I could ever hope or imagine. You are a great brother, and I love you very much. Thanks for always being there for me.

WHITNEY

The thief comes only to steal and kill and destroy; I have come that they may have life, and have it to the full.
—John 10:10

You are so special to me. I love you and am so thankful you are my sister. I want you to know that John 10:10 has been the most important verse to me in recent years. It has been a verse I turn to when I am in need of encouragement. It is a verse that fills me with an eternal purpose. It is a verse that excites me and gives me energy. It is a verse that provides me with a challenge, and serves as a reality check from time to time.

Jesus came so that we may have life, a life of abundance. In my view, living life to the full for Jesus means living each and every day with purpose. It means squeezing every ounce of every second that you are on this earth breathing and living. Life to the full means taking nothing for granted, fighting through every trial that seeks to kill and destroy you. Life to the full means laughing, loving, and being thankful for each day you have been given. Whitney, you are full of life.

I have never met anyone who can make me laugh so hard, with such ease. Your stories, your jokes, your antics, and your spunky personality, all bring a smile to my face. Your text messages, your animal noises, and your work stories, all make me smile and laugh. You have never met a stranger in your life and you can always find a reason to start a conversation. I know I am not alone in saying this, but when I finish interacting with you, I leave smiling and laughing.

I truly admire your imagination and your willingness to be goofy. I tend to think that I can be creative and have a decent imagination. Yet you put me to shame. Your imagination is out of this world, and is such a blessing. I love talking with you because I never know where the conversation is going to go. I love hanging out with you because you bring a peace and assurance that says to me, "It is OK to be goofy." I love that when I am with you, you display an immense amount of confidence that says, "I don't care what other people think, I am going to be myself, and I am going to have fun." That confidence is absolutely thrilling to see in you. And I love that when I am with you, your confidence increases my confidence. Being around you enables me to be a more confident person, and enables me to be myself.

Whitney, you are a model of strength, character, and perseverance. Your strength and determination day in and day out provide me with energy and purpose. You have been called to run a difficult race, but your character does not allow you to quit. You have chosen to persevere rather than give up. You have shown me how to live life abundantly. Your smile, your laughter, and your bubbly personality make you a joy to be around.

On numerous occasions since being in Germany, I have been asked two questions. The first is: Whom do you miss most from America? Without hesitation the answer to the first question is always "my sister." I have missed being around you and seeing you. Every year on March 19, as well as so many other days, I wish more than anything else that I could be hanging out with you.

The second question I have faced many times from a variety of people is: Does your family support your being in Germany? To answer this question I always refer to a note you wrote me as I was boarding the plane for the very first time. Tears always come to my eyes as I say, "Whitney said to me that she is sad to see me go, but she is excited for the BFA students. She said that she was excited for the students because she knows I will be a brother/friend/coach to them, just as I have been a brother/friend to her. Knowing that, she is very excited for what the students will be getting when my plane lands in Germany." Those words you wrote have always stayed with me. They fill me with love, encouragement, and excitement.

You are a phenomenal sister and I am so blessed for what God has given me in you. Your life is a living testimony to God's provision and love. If I can somehow obtain a quarter of the courage, strength, and perseverance you have, I will be beyond excited. I love you.

CONTENTS

Acknowledgments xix

Introduction xxi

Mile 1: Courage 1
Mile 2: Discipline 7
Mile 3: Patience 15
Mile 4: Freedom 23
Mile 5: Goals 29
Mile 6: Companionship 35
Mile 7: Loneliness 43
Mile 8: Persistence 53
Mile 9: Excitement 63
Mile 10: Adaptability 73
Mile 11: Strength 81
Mile 12: Trust 91
Mile 13: Insanity 101
Mile 14: Focus 109
Mile 15: Pain 117
Mile 16: Dedication 129
Mile 17: Worship 141

Mile 18: Anticipation 151
Mile 19: Endurance. 159
Mile 20: Tenacity. 167
Mile 21: Encouragement. 175
Mile 22: Exhaustion 189
Mile 23: Perseverance 197
Mile 24: Gratitude. 207
Mile 25: Resolve 213
Mile 26: Joy. 221

Endnotes. 229

ACKNOWLEDGMENTS

A MARATHON RUNNER depends on the volunteers at the aid stations for encouragement, refreshment, instruction, and help. In the same way, I have greatly benefited from a team of family and friends who rallied around me to make this dream a reality. I could not have completed this book without their many hours of tedious editing, encouraging words, insight, and love. I owe many thanks to those who have been running alongside me in this project.

To David Harrop, you have been a shepherd to the flock of BFCF for many years. I am thankful to have learned from you for four years. Your heart seeks God, and your life shows that. Thank you for not only being my pastor, but my friend.

To Katrina Custer, we share a love for missions, history, running, and cooking. If only we could agree on a football team! Because of your careful eye I finally have a vague idea of how to appropriately use a comma. Each chapter that passed through your hands came back ten times better. Thank you for your many hours of tedious editing. Go Pack Go!

To Brittany Leuenberger, you have edited my writing ever since freshman year in college. You continually take something rough and choppy and turn it into something worthy of reading. I appreciate all your time, effort, and input. Above all, I am thankful that with you and Josiah, I know I have great friends for life.

To Mike Dreves, not only a coach, but a friend. I know the many late hours you spend in your office working to make your program better. You are not only producing better soccer players, but helping boys turn into men of integrity. Thank you for all the conversations and advice along the way.

To Jim and Lynn Patterson, even amongst all of our "fights" I knew we had a great friendship. Lynn, you always asked me questions not because you were nosy, but because you cared. Because of that I was able to share my heart, and I appreciated and needed that more than you will know. Jim, you are a phenomenal friend and running partner. Your encouragement and enthusiasm lifted my spirits for miles upon miles. You made the Freiburg marathon such an incredible day. I look forward to running Boston with you someday.

To all my fellow Sonneknights, you may not be mentioned by name, but you were very influential in the writing. Thank you for all the years together in the dorm, and the memories we created. The first floor will always be a very special place to me. Never forget how much God loves you. Go and change the world for Christ.

To Ross, Croce, Manny, Jack, Schlebby, Free, Caleb, AJ, and Bear, as iron sharpens iron so one man sharpens another. Thank you for sharpening me and being there for me. You guys are amazing. Thank you for being my companions and for carrying me. Many of the characteristics within this book I first saw in you. Now, because of you, they are starting to grow in me. Thank you.

To my grandparents, your prayers have showered me for years. I appreciate all of your wisdom, insight, and love.

To the reader, thank you for the opportunity to share with you my race. I pray it proves helpful as you run your race.

To my Lord and Savior, Jesus Christ. Thank you for giving us life, and life abundantly. Thank you for promising never to leave us nor forsake us.

INTRODUCTION

"**C**OME ON TOM Tom; lace 'em up! We are going to go on a run that would make Reggie White proud!"

Though merely eleven years old, the words were powerful coming off of my dad's tongue as they hit my ears. I was filled with excitement, joy, and nervousness, among other emotions I was too young to fully recognize or identify. I had often seen my dad take off from our house for a run. I very clearly knew when he returned from a winter run, per the poignant stench that came wafting through the house. I had even been on the sideline as I cheered my dad to one of his completed marathons. Yet until then, seldom was there a time in which I was invited to run alongside him, let alone a run worthy of the name Reggie White. At the time, Reggie was an All Pro football player for the Green Bay Packers who was celebrated for partaking in rigorous workouts to maintain peak condition. I had the excitement and joy of being able to run with my dad, fear and nervousness for the intensity of what I was about to endure, butterflies from the mixed bag of emotions, and butterflies from the adventure of the unknown. *One run, many thoughts.*

I ventured on my first of many "Reggie White runs" as an eleven-year-old boy trying to be cool and keep up with his dad. Little did I know that he would lead me up what we called "Hospital Hill" not once, not twice, but three times. Hospital Hill led to the entrance of the local area hospital. I like to think the name "Hospital Hill" originated not because of its proximity to the hospital, but because by the time you were one-third of the way up, you thought you were going to die. By the time you reached the entrance to the hospital you were about halfway up the hill, contemplating making a quick right and admitting yourself into the emergency ward. And when you made it to the top … indescribable joy. *One run, many thoughts.*

The running terrain changes over time as well as the purposes of the runs. At some point we moved 1,500 miles across the country. Instead of Hospital Hill, there was Stratham Hill. (I think my dad had a masochistic love of running hills. Thank goodness we didn't live in Colorado.) The purpose was no longer to complete a "Reggie White workout." And it was no longer me running in the shadows of my father. Stratham Hill remains in my mind as a place where I ran side by side with my dad to encourage, motivate, and challenge a father who was battling a disease—the dreaded "C" word—that threatened to destroy his body. It was no longer I who was in the shadow, but now my mentor, my friend, and my inspiration was in *my* shadow. These runs were characterized by an attitude of perseverance, courage, dedication, and pain. What once was, was no longer. What once could, could no more. *One run, many thoughts.*

Time pushed us forward, and the hills on the East Coast were replaced by, as Dr. Martin Luther King Jr. described them, "the heightening hills of Pennsylvania." Moving away for college meant I no longer had my long-time running partner. Yet through college athletics I established new friendships and new running partners. Growth occurred from the spreading of my own wings and flying on my own. The rolling hills of Pennsylvania drew forth companionship, freedom from the classroom and academic studies, and discipline. During my college years I stepped into a world previously unknown to me, the world of training and completing my first marathon (26.2 miles). *One run, many thoughts.*

After college, the terrain changed once again. Ministry brought me across the Atlantic Ocean to the trails and wooded areas

INTRODUCTION

of Germany's Black Forest region. Unfortunately, I once again encountered hills, and wondered why it seemed that I never got the opportunity to run on flat ground. Since I was no longer actively playing on a competitive athletic team, running morphed from something I had to do to stay in shape into something I got to do simply because I loved to do it. As I embraced a new continent full of foreign cultures and let go of all that was comfortable, normal, and known, runs became marked by loneliness, endurance, and adaptability. The desire to grow not only as a person but as a runner brought forth runs containing resolve, focus, and goals. Running provided extended periods of worship, through laughter, joy, and as Eric Liddle so brilliantly stated, "by feeling his pleasure." Worship also came through tears, runs of crying out begging for answers, guidance, and companionship. The Black Forest provided beautiful scenery while training for my second and third marathon (42.2 kilometers). *One run, many thoughts.*

    Running not only holds benefits for our physical bodies, but equally proves beneficial for our minds and hearts. A single run can generate and hold a plethora of thoughts and emotions. Legend states that the ancient Greek messenger Pheidippides ran 25 miles from the battlefield near Marathon to Athens to deliver news of a Greek military victory. From this we have the beginning of the modern day marathon (though there have been slight variations throughout the years). Although Pheidippides and we run centuries apart from each other, the common denominator remains that one run carries many thoughts.

    My desire is to share and experience with you the many thoughts, emotions, and attributes that are often generated over the 26.2 miles of a marathon. For each mile we encounter, we will unearth and focus on a thought, feeling, emotion, or trait that would likely occur during that specific mile in the race. While doing so, we will consider different biblical characters along the way who also found themselves dealing with similar types of thoughts, feelings, emotions, or traits.

    Whether you are a first-time runner looking to start a new habit, or a world-class athlete who has conquered the running world many times over, it is my prayer that this book unites your passion to run and your passion to serve our Lord Jesus Christ. One run, many thoughts.

Father in heaven, I thank you for this journey we are about to take. I am thankful you are with us every step of the way. Through the valleys, up the hills, and at the mountaintop, Lord, you are there with us. Guiding us. Protecting us. Changing us. May the race we are running be one that helps us become more like you. Amen.

MILE 1
COURAGE

"The miracle isn't that I finished. The miracle is that I had the courage to start."
—John Bingham

"Success is not final, failure is not fatal: it is the courage to continue that counts."
—Winston Churchill

"When they saw the courage of Peter and John and realized that they were unschooled, ordinary men, they were astonished and they took note that these men had been with Jesus."
—Acts 4:13

WRITING THE FIRST lines of a book have proven to be quite intimidating. A plethora of ideas have been swirling around for months, notes have been taken, outlines drawn, and then it is time for it to all start. It is time for the ink to hit the paper. Up until now it seems as though every idea was positive and encouraging. Every note taken and every brainstorm jotted down gushed with endless possibilities. Yet now, the blank page stands as a terrifying force of opposition. The notes that once held so much fruit and energy look frail in the shadows of doubt, uncertainty, and fear. The task once seemed so simple and was met with energy. The lack of words on the page have taken the wind out of the sail. What must be done to change the situation? What action is integral to overcoming the obstacle? Courage. A mind and heart in possession of the ability to face adversity, danger, and challenge. Courage is not simply the fortitude to face the situation, but the resolve to do so without fear, and with a confident and unabashed spirit. Courage. I am in need of courage as I sit to type my heart and my thoughts. You may be in need of courage as you begin to run your race.

The starting line of a race of any distance, especially a marathon, can be intimidating. For months you prepare your body and mind. You outline and meticulously follow a training regimen. Notes on running smart, proper hydration, and the best recovery methods have been taken. You have dreamed and rehearsed in your mind breaking the tape and crossing the finish line. Yet now the starting line is under your feet; it is time for the race to begin. The task of a run once seemed so simple and was met with energy; now the thought of running for 26.2 miles leaves you with a lump in your stomach. Voices of doubt enter your head, drowning out the cheers of the crowd, causing you to question whether you trained hard enough or if your stretching routine was adequate. Yet here you stand, no choice but to run forward. No opportunity to turn back.

What mindset is integral to overcoming the obstacle that lays 26.2 miles ahead of you? Courage. A mind and heart that is ready to tackle the challenges you face. Confidence and a spirit that

COURAGE

stands on the starting line, smiles, and looks forward to crossing the finish line. Run your race with courage.

The Bible is filled with men and women who exemplified what it means to be courageous. Upon hearing the mocking cries of Goliath, David decided to put an end to the jesting of the Philistine and stand up for his people. Filled with confidence and courage, David did not hesitate in the face of affliction; rather, he ran to the battlefield.[1] Courage enables us to run toward the battle.

Joshua and Caleb returned from spying on the land promised to them certain of what they had seen, but more convinced of their God who had sent them. The other ten spies who gave an account before them trembled with fear, and a lack of confidence rattled their trust. In front of the entire Israelite community, Joshua and Caleb courageously silenced the people and encouraged them to take possession of the land. The news of the other ten, however, caused the Israelites to raise their voices and weep loudly. They eventually schemed a plan to stone the leaders and return to Egypt under new authority. Courageously, in the face of difficulty, peer pressure, and a weeping nation, Joshua and Caleb remained convinced of who God said he was.[2] Courage empowers us to speak truth when others are afraid to.

Esther was a woman of strength and courage. Despite her prominent position as queen, her life was at risk due to the evil plans of Haman. Not only was Esther's life at risk, but her entire family and all of the Jews within Xerxes' kingdom were days away from being executed. Knowing that one wrong move, one phrase incorrectly stated, could end her life, she walked into the presence of King Xerxes with courage. Having spent days fasting and praying, she courageously walked through the palace doors knowing that she had been raised for that specific time and purpose. If it meant her life, so be it. She was going to courageously run the race she was called to run.[3] Courage readies us to stand up for what we believe to be right.

In Acts chapter 2, we find two men who were specifically noted because of the courage they displayed. Following the Holy Spirit falling at Pentecost, the early church was filled with enthusiasm and fervor to preach to anyone and everyone. Peter and John spoke, healed, addressed crowds, enjoyed fellowship with other believers, and furiously upset the religious elite. The priests, extremely frustrated by the message the two were preaching, had them seized and thrown into jail.

I wonder what the conversation between Peter and John sounded like as they sat on the floor of their prison cell. If it were me, I would have most likely thrown in the towel, looked at the cold walls surrounding me, believing it was time to pack up, and given in. Were they flooded with thoughts of bitterness? It was not too long ago they had found themselves surrounded by a multitude of other believers, receiving the Holy Spirit and speaking in a multitude of languages, with everyone amazed and perplexed. They left that room on fire, and where had it gotten them? In a cold, musty, dark, prison cell. Could we blame them if they were to give up? They had spent years following a man who they believed was going to bring about the rise of a nation, only to see him crucified. They gathered in a room with multitudes of believers and received the Holy Spirit, only to have that room replaced by an uncomfortable dark prison cell. Yet they responded far differently than many would expect; full of fervor, passion, and, above all, courage.

How do you find yourself responding to the situations life throws at you? More than likely, most of us have not experienced the walls of a physical prison as a result of our religious beliefs. Yet how many of us have been imprisoned by fear and worry? What was your response when the stress of hearing the words "the tumor is cancerous" imprisoned your family? Some may be able to look back at life situations and assess how they responded in the past. We can all look ahead knowing the evil one is scheming how he might imprison us next. It has been said, "You are either about to enter a storm, are in the middle of a storm, or are just coming out of a storm." Get courageous, and get ready to get wet!

The day after being thrown in jail, Peter and John were momentarily taken out of their prison cell and given an opportunity to state their case and defend themselves. This was their opportunity to stand before the religious elite and say, "We are sorry. You were right; we were wrong. It won't happen again." They had the opportunity to save their own necks rather than face further imprisonment. Naturally they took the safe and easy road, right? Not at all. That could not be further from the truth of what actually happened. Rather than view imprisonment and their court appearance as a disruption to their ministry, they viewed it as an added bonus and a unique opportunity to further what they had already been doing. In reading Peter's response to his audience, it sounds less and less like an apology, and more and more like a sermon.[4] Leaving those in attendance with one simple, yet amazing, conclusion: Peter and John were filled with courage because they had rubbed shoulders with Jesus.

Peter and John walked with Jesus, and as a result their lives were radically changed. So radical was the change that those who watched the way they conducted themselves, and heard the way in which they spoke, had no other option but to be astonished. Peter and John were not the cream-of-the-crop graduates from the finest seminary in town. They were unschooled. Ordinary. Average Joes. Nobodies. Yet through them, and through others with even fewer credentials, they changed the entire Roman Empire. Why? Because they received courage from walking with Jesus.

May the same be said of me and you. May your sons and daughters be guided by moms and dads who do not flinch when a Goliath-sized problem stalks your family. Pray that your boss will recognize your courage when you speak the truth regardless of what the other board members say. Courageously stand up for what you believe in, knowing what it may cost you. When the difficulties of this life threaten to imprison you, may you courageously let your faith be evident in your lifestyle.

It does not take a flashy suit, a seminary degree, or a position of power. It takes a life that has been radically changed by time spent with Jesus Christ, and a mind and heart in possession of the ability to face adversity, danger, and challenge. Courage is not simply the fortitude to face the situation, but the resolve to do so without fear, and with a confident and unabashed spirit.

Father in heaven, thank you for the examples of your children who lived lives full of courage. Thank you for providing strength to the weak, comfort to the broken-hearted, and peace to the weary. May our journey be one marked by courage. May our lives be radically changed, and the lives of those around us, because they recognize that we have spent time with you. Amen.

MILE 2
DISCIPLINE

"Champions do not become champions when they win the event, but in the hours, weeks, months, and years they spend preparing for it. The victorious performance itself is merely the demonstration of their championship character."
—T. Alan Armstrong

"With self-discipline most anything is possible."
—Theodore Roosevelt

"Now when Daniel learned that the decree had been published, he went home to his upstairs room where the windows opened toward Jerusalem. Three times a day he got down on his knees and prayed, giving thanks to his God, just as he had done before."
—Daniel 6:10

*I*T WAS CLOSE to seven-thirty in the morning, the sun had yet to crest the German hills, and the temperature failed to climb past -7 degrees Celsius. I startled my friends by giving them a loud "good morning" as I passed by. It was not so much the presence of somebody that startled them, nor was it someone speaking English in rural Germany. It was more that I was a solid fifteen miles from home, a few layers on top, shorts on bottom, and running. Some may think that running in the middle of January is foolish. On some days I can hardly disagree. But on this particular morning I thought I was pretty smart for how prepared I was. After all, I had those cheap "expose to the air" pocket warmers in each hand. I was feeling warm and smart until the pocket warmers died and my sweat started to freeze.

My friends were on their way to work, and I would soon meet them there, albeit their mode of transportation was a car while my vehicle was my legs. It was early, dark, and cold. My bed had been warm, inviting, and peaceful. Yet there I was, far from my heated room and comfortable bed, feeling the chilly wind hit my nearly numb skin. A part of me really did not want to be running at that point in time, but deep down I was fully aware that if I were to have dreams of finishing a marathon, this was part of the price I would have to pay.

Being dedicated to something will most often not be enough to carry you through. You must obtain a method to obtain obedience. You must practice. You must prepare. You must exercise self-control. When all of these are combined, they create discipline, which is a vital part of training for a marathon and living a life worthy of the calling of Jesus Christ.

By now you are in Mile 2. The fun is just beginning.

If you have already completed a marathon or any other endurance event, I commend you. If you are currently enduring the training regimen, I commend you as well. There are spectators who show up on race day thinking the race was completed in the four hours or so it took you to finish that day's race. Don't let them fool you. The real race is the journey that brings you to the start and eventually to the finish line.

DISCIPLINE

I believe that only those who have actually trained for a marathon or similar endurance event truly understand the discipline, sacrifice, time, and energy that is required. It takes discipline to forgo that second serving of food, no matter how good Grandma's homemade meatloaf may be. It takes discipline to refrain from going out with friends, knowing a good night's sleep will help carry you through the eighteen miles your next day of training will bring. It takes discipline to plan ahead and prepare for something that is weeks or months away. It takes practice, preparation, self-control, and self-command. Running the race requires discipline.

Put running aside for a second. Stop thinking about training, and think about life. How disciplined are you? How much self-control, obedience, and self-command do you have? Have you ever said to yourself, "I wish I were as disciplined in my spiritual life as I am with _____ (fill in the blank)"? Am I the only one who falls asleep at night and begs for forgiveness after realizing I found a way to wake up early to run, but the following day slept in and neglected to pray to my Creator and Savior? How would our lives differ if we were dedicated to prayer? In what ways would the lives of our neighbors change if we were disciplined to pray for and encourage them? What if our discipline in our relationship with Jesus Christ exceeded the discipline we apply to our training?

When we examine the life of Daniel, we find a man who was disciplined. His self-control, practice, and preparation provided him with the tools he needed to survive a multitude of difficult situations that came roaring at him. The situations you face may be clothed differently than the ones Daniel faced, but hopefully your discipline is cut from the same cloth.

When we first meet Daniel, his country had just been besieged. The temple had been ransacked and its treasures were stolen and placed in the temples of a distant country to honor foreign and false gods. Adding insult to injury, Daniel and a few others were taken captive and forced to learn the language and customs of their captor, Babylon. New country. New language. New customs. Same Daniel. Same discipline.

Daniel was a man of discipline. When he entered this chapter in his life, many new things came his way, most of which he had no control over. His housing, education and occupation were jammed down his throat by the Babylonians. He was provided with only a certain type of food and drink every day. When commanded to partake in the palace food and wine, he refused out of a desire to refrain from defiling himself. Unclean, tarnished, dirty, rendered impure, and corrupt. That is what would have happened to Daniel had he been defiled by the king's food and wine. To avoid this, Daniel disciplined himself over a ten-day period to encounter a strict diet. Diets are not easy to accomplish. Diets are not easy to maintain. Don't believe me? Simply go to a local bookstore and browse the nutrition section. Take a few minutes to jot down how many different books there are about dieting. You may get a headache simply by trying to determine which diet you are going to go on, and then which book will be the most beneficial to you. If you are more into technology, take a second to browse through all the apps that are available when you search the word "diet." Many people strive to go on a diet; few have the discipline it takes to complete it.

Daniel and a few of his prison mates embarked on this diet so they might not be defiled, and God blessed their obedience and discipline. After the ten-day period, Daniel and his friends looked healthy. In fact, they looked better than the other men who had been feasting on the king's royal foods. At first, those over Daniel scratched their heads because he had decided to choose God's way rather than the "normal way." Afterward, those over Daniel turned their heads because God's way resulted in something above and beyond what they thought possible. Through this episode Daniel's foundation of trust in God and trust in his fellow countrymen were set in stone. New country. New language. New food. Same Daniel. Same discipline.

By his trustworthiness, uprightness, and diligence, Daniel climbed the ranks of the elite within Babylon. After a few years and a few interpreted dreams, Belshazzar, the Babylonian king, clothed Daniel in purple and proclaimed him to be the third highest ruler in the entire kingdom. After Belshazzar's death, the new king, Darius, intended to set Daniel over the entire kingdom. What a ride this must have been for Daniel. Not long before this promotion, his country and temple were being pillaged; now he was set to be placed in the highest possible position. Things finally appeared to be taking a turn for the better until Darius's satraps got involved.

The satraps were in essence Darius's political posse, his group of followers who would do anything and everything for their king. In their eyes, Daniel had become a man they loved to hate. Everything he did, every dream he interpreted, and every piece of wisdom he gave made their blood boil. Perhaps they were fearful that a foreigner had been placed in such a high position; particularly a foreigner who only a few years prior had seen his country wiped away. Maybe they were jealous Daniel was in a position they all secretly craved. For whatever reason, they did not want Daniel at the top, so they conceived a plan to destroy him.

Perhaps one of Darius's satraps said to the other, "Did you see him take money from the treasury and put it towards his retirement fund?" Didn't happen. Daniel was trustworthy. Another man in jealousy offered, "I heard Daniel took pleasure in the king's daughters to get to his high position." Not this Daniel. He was pure and upright. Finally a different satrap blurted out, "I saw Daniel clock in late and check out early, yet still demand his full paycheck." Wrong again. Daniel was praised for being diligent and honorable. The satraps scratched their heads, most likely the same way Daniel's former prison guard scratched his head when Daniel showed up from his diet looking healthier and fitter than those who indulged in the palace's delicacies. They could not find a way to defile his character, but they would not give up. Could our world use a few more Christians who set an example by doing good, so that those who oppose us may be ashamed because they have nothing bad to say about us?[5]

The satraps had another idea. They had been stalking Daniel for days, trying to find something indecent they could pin on him, yet had not thought of the obvious. It was reported that at least three times a day Daniel retreated to his upper room to pray.

RUNNING THROUGH LIFE

Aware of how they could imprison Daniel, they approached Darius and persuaded him to issue a decree. Of course, the decree was presented in a way that made it appear as though it was honoring and glorifying Darius, when in fact they were only concerned with leading Daniel to the slaughter. Little did they realize that when the evil one thinks he can lead a lamb to the slaughter, through God, the lamb returns with something far greater than ever anticipated.

Daniel heard the decree. He knew the implications it could have on his life. He remembered a decree that had been put forth not too long earlier by Nebuchadnezzar that had forced Shadrach, Meshach, and Abednego into a hot situation. New king. New decree. Same Daniel. Same God. Same discipline. Three times a day, he retreated to his room to pray.

Time to get away from the busyness of the palace. Time to get away from the corruption and evil he rubbed shoulders with. Time to be still. Time to praise. Time to ask for help. Time to focus. Time to talk. Time to listen. Daniel needed this time in order to be all that God had called him to be. Daniel needed a disciplined prayer life. So do I. So do you. Daniel recognized the need for his time of prayer, and there was not a thing that was going to get in the way of that. Neither mobs of satraps nor a royal decree could interrupt his prayer time.

At a quick glance one might actually walk away from this point of the story discouraged and put off. After all, what did Daniel receive for being a man of discipline in prayer? A pat on the back from his buddies? A corporate membership to the local country club? A cushioned seat in the front row pew at the temple? No, no, and no. He was given what was meant to be a one-way ticket into a den of lions. Yet what man meant for evil, God meant for good.

From Daniel's trust, obedience, and discipline, God was praised. Daniel was rescued from the mouths of the hungry lions and he immediately praised God. After addressing King Darius, the first words out of his mouth heaped praises for how God rescued and delivered. As a result of Daniel living a life of discipline and obedience, he influenced the lives of those around him. So much so that the king issued a new decree, stating:

DISCIPLINE

… [T]hat in every part of my kingdom people must fear and reverence the God of Daniel: For he is the living God and he endures forever; his kingdom will not be destroyed, his dominion will never end. He rescues and he saves; he performs signs and wonders in the heavens and on the earth. He has rescued Daniel from the power of the lions.[6]

Same Daniel. Same God. Same discipline. A changed kingdom.

In Paul's second letter to Timothy, he reminded Timothy that the Spirit of God does not make us timid, but gives us power, love, and self-discipline.[7] Daniel was a man characterized by discipline. We too must be men and women defined by discipline. This discipline must not only be evident in our marathon training and the race itself, it must be exhibited in our daily life with Christ.

Jesus, you are the same yesterday, today, and forever. For that we thank you. You are patient, loving, merciful, and full of grace. You are the same. Lord, we ask that our actions and our decisions would do nothing but bring you glory and honor. Create in us a discipline that resembles that of Daniel. Whenever things around us heat up, may we find ourselves grounded in you. Whenever we find ourselves in a den of lions, may your presence surround us and bring us peace. You are good, Lord. You are good. Thank you. Amen.

MILE 3
PATIENCE

"Concentrate on small segments of your race at a time. For example, rather than obsessing about the distance that remains, simply complete the next mile in good form … try another, then another, until the race is done."
—Jerry Lynch

"One chance is all you need."
—Jesse Owens

"Therefore, seeing we also are compassed about by so great a cloud of witnesses, let us lay aside every weight, and the sin which doth so easily beset us, and let us run with patience the race that is set before us."
—Hebrews 12:1

AS I SIT down to start writing this chapter, I find myself working and living in Germany in a boarding school dormitory that houses twenty-one boys in grades nine to twelve. Composing this chapter has been on my mind and heart for a long while, and I have struggled to find the words I desire to put on paper. Why? Simply because I know that in the past few days, my actions and my heart have preached a message of anything but patience. It would be easier to just write down everything I have done, every way I have lost patience, become frustrated, and unleashed my annoyance, and say, "Don't do what I have done."

This is how my morning started. I woke up earlier than I really wanted in order to prepare breakfast. With no grace whatsoever, I pulled an egg out of its carton, allowing it to slip right through my fingers. Out of pure reaction my other hand swung down to catch the falling object without giving any thought to the fact that the object testing the laws of gravity was a fragile egg. My hand provided the egg no cushion at all; rather, it served as a landing pad that was begging to be decorated in yolk. After washing my hand, I reached into the cabinet to grab a towel, only to shut the drawer while leaving my hand still inside. A bruised and purple thumb was my medal of clumsiness.

Deep inside I was wishing I could crawl back into bed and hit the "restart" button. I had already been through more than I wanted to encounter the entire day. Things were not starting on the right foot, but a nice, hearty breakfast would fill my stomach and provide the energy needed to get over a difficult morning … or so I thought. Reaching into the tray that held the forks, I found that someone had spilled half a bottle of pancake syrup in it, leaving every fork sticky. At that point I ran out of patience.

So far I have been using the dictionary to help me define the key word for each chapter. But I did not want to find a definition that might further expose the fact that I had been living in direct contrast to the virtue of patience. So I decided to poll some of the students I live with to see how they would define patience. Their answers were both profound and entertaining:

"Doing something consistently even when it is not easy or fun."

"Controlling your emotions."

"Putting up with my mom when she constantly bugs me."

"Love."

"When you are in a car and you really need to go to the bathroom, but you keep going so you don't have to wake up the person who is sleeping. That is patience!"

"Putting up with stuff you don't deserve, but choosing not to retaliate."

"When your sister gets on your nerves and you don't yell at her … wait … patience is how long you let your sister annoy you before you get mad."

Being patient requires us to maintain our composure when things annoy, provoke, delay, or disturb us. It may sound simple and easy on paper, but practicing and exemplifying these are quite difficult. Practicing patience while running can be as challenging as living out the virtue in other areas of your life. Being a patient runner will reap you great rewards, starting with your training, carrying you through the early miles of the race, and into the final stretch.

You are not going to build the endurance to run a marathon overnight. You are not going to qualify for the Boston Marathon after a week's worth of training. Rome was not built in a day; neither was your running capability. Most training programs encourage you to train for at least sixteen weeks prior to running a marathon. Be patient while training. Trust your training. If you run through the training too quickly, you are more susceptible to picking up an injury and hindering your chances of finishing.

Being patient with yourself is also important during your training. In a bizarre way, sometimes it is much easier for me to show other people patience, while I fail to show myself patience. One poor run where I struggle to control my breathing, or one hill that affects me more than usual, and I struggle to forgive myself and show myself the patience I need.

This point was recently made obvious to me as I struggled to complete what was supposed to be an easy twelve-mile run. The run was one I had been anxiously waiting for and was at the tail end of my training. In fact, it was my last scheduled double-digit run prior to my third marathon. The sun was shining and the air was warm, showing promise that for the first time in my months of training it might be warm enough for me to wear short sleeves. And, I had a former student who was going to bike along with me for the run. For the majority of my training, I had been doing all of the runs on my own, but if possible on long runs, I tried to find somebody who would be willing to ride a bike along the way. Bikers help me run at a steady pace, help encourage me when I feel tired, keep me entertained with conversation, and, most importantly, carry my water!

Jessica willingly agreed to be my trainer and biking companion for the day. I wish I could say I was fast, impressive, and light on my feet. Not this time. It was long, hard, and tiring. I continually muttered to myself under my breath, trying to get out of my funk. It was useless. It had been months since we had seen each other, so Jessica and I had some catching up to do. She had recently moved back to the U.S. and it had not been an easy transition. Loneliness, frustration, and uncertainty all crept in and derailed her.

About seven miles into the run, Jessica leaned over and said to me, "I have realized that I simply need to be more patient with myself; not be so hard and be willing to show myself grace." If the difficulty of the run wasn't enough to blow me away, the truth she was speaking into my heart certainly pushed me over.

Be patient. Endure the pain, bear the frustration, and show yourself grace without losing your temper or becoming increasingly irritated. I encourage you to be patient in your training. Be patient when you have an off day, when you struggle to complete all of the miles of your scheduled long runs. Be patient. You have plenty of time to do what you need to do.

In the same manner, be patient during your marathon, especially in the early miles. As you approach the Mile 3 marker, keep in mind that you have more than twenty miles to go. Be patient.

PATIENCE

It is not uncommon to be boxed in during the first few miles of a race. For example, if you hope to maintain a steady eight-minute-per-mile pace, do not be surprised if during the first few miles you can't clock anything under nine minutes. There are often lots of people on the road with the space being quite limited. Do not become agitated by your inability to hit your stride. Enjoy this time with those around you. Later in the race you will find that you have lost some of the community and the encouragement that comes while running in a crowd. If you are going slower than you would like, you probably have more breath than you are accustomed to. So use that breath and make friends. Chat with the runners surrounding you. Encourage them.

While running in the mass of people at the start of a race, I like to recite to myself the opening verse of Hebrews chapter 12: "Therefore since we are surrounded by such a great cloud of witnesses ..."[8] In Hebrews chapter 11, the author highlighted some of the great men and women of faith. I am in no way saying that the crowd of runners compares to that which we will experience in heaven, but it can serve as a sneak peak. In the early stages of the race you will find yourself surrounded by many others who, like you, have put in the hours, miles, headaches, and sacrifice to be there with you. Whether you know them by name or not, and whether you speak the same language or not, you have come together to that one place for the same cause, and it is a thrilling thing.

As you are in the middle of all those witnesses, make sure you don't judge them. My first marathon was the Walt Disney World Marathon in Orlando, Florida. The atmosphere was phenomenal; plenty of fans, amazing organization, and many entertaining runners. Many runners wore costumes. One woman was dressed up as Minnie Mouse. Within these early miles of being boxed in, I found myself running alongside Minnie, and in a surge of impatience muttering, "How can *I* be running next to a woman dressed up as Minnie Mouse? This shouldn't be happening." So in an impatient rage I picked up my pace and sped past her, bumping shoulders with other runners as I tried to distance myself from Minnie. For a while, it seemed like it was the correct decision. Twenty miles later, I hit the wall. (We will talk about "the wall" in later chapters.) Tired, struggling, and cramping in every possible place, I struggled to finish the race. As I regained some strength by the last water station, I envied the runners who were running by with relative ease and smiles on their faces. Striving to find some encouragement from their examples, I began trotting along once again, only to soon be passed by, you guessed it, Minnie Mouse. She finished ahead of me, and I humbly learned an important lesson—be patient. If I had been patient rather than worrying about what I looked like, or how I compared to the runners around me, I would have run better that day.

After I asked my students how they would define patience, I asked them whom they would cite as good biblical characters who exemplified the virtue. Job was a common answer, as he showed patience in his many trials. Jacob also received a few votes for the way in which he worked for fourteen years to be Rachel's husband, and to him "they seemed like a day."[9]

One of the responses surprised me: Paul. Certainly Paul had courage, enthusiasm, wisdom, and strength; yet patience would not be on the top of my list of Paul's attributes. When I asked why this answer was given, a short sentence was all that was needed to once again blow me away: "He loved so many people, and wrote them letters. They gave him so many reasons to be mad and to want to give up, but he did not; he always continued to love them."

Paul exemplified patience. Paul continued to love when it would have been perfectly understandable, in our minds, to give up. As we look through the many letters he wrote, we can continually see his love and his patience. Look at the way in which he addresses the churches.

To the church in Rome:

> I thank my God through Jesus Christ for all of you, because your faith is being reported all over the world. God, whom I serve in my spirit in preaching the gospel of his Son, is my witness how constantly I remember you in my prayers at all times; and I pray that now at last by God's will the way may be opened for me to come to you.[10]

PATIENCE

To the church in Corinth:

I always thank my God for you because of his grace given you in Christ Jesus.[11]

When Paul first wrote to the church of Corinth and encouraged the people to better understand love, the first adjective he used was the word "patient."[12]

These churches and the individuals Paul served alongside were not the easiest people to get along with. I imagine most of us can relate very closely to that. Despite their shortcomings and failures, he continued to show them patience. Through his continual acts of praying, writing, and loving, Paul exemplified patience.

We are unaware of the response given back to Paul. Sometimes I wish we could read what the church in Corinth said when it responded to Paul. I wonder how many times Paul heard the words, "We are sorry, we messed up again." Or "Paul, we are trying to rid ourselves of this sin but we keep failing." Paul's response? He patiently reminded them they were going through a transformation, and that God is faithful.

Jesus is patient with us when we come before him broken in recognition of our sin and say, "I am sorry, Lord. I am a sinner. Please forgive me." Paul was not willing to give up on these churches. He was patient with them and desired to grow with them through their transformation.

For a good while, my hand still carried the stench of egg yolk and the size of my finger had increased as a result of being smashed in the drawer. Thankfully, that is not the only thing that has grown. Through God's grace, he has allowed me to increase the amount of patience I have and show. While I desire to cultivate the patience I show to myself and those around me, I am forever thankful for the way in which God has been patient with me. Do you find it amazing that he has not given up on us yet?

Daily I fail to live up to God's standards, yet he chooses to love me despite my failures. The churches to whom Paul was writing gave him plenty of reason to give up, to be mad, or to become frustrated. By responding with patience, Paul not only acted as an excellent example, but also showed us a picture of God's heart.

Father, you are so patient with your children. Thank you for being the greatest example of one who exhibits patience. Jesus, your servant Paul has encouraged us to be patient with others, as well as ourselves. In so doing may we show the world a love they have never seen before, and may we change the world through our patient love. One step at a time, one mile at a time. Thank you, Lord. Amen.

MILE 4
FREEDOM

"Running gives freedom. When you run you can determine your own tempo. You can choose your own course and think whatever you want.
Nobody tells you what to do."
—Nina Kuscik

"I loved the feeling of freedom in running, the fresh air, the feeling that the only person I'm competing with is me."
—Wilma Rudloph

"Though your sins are like scarlet, they shall be as white as snow; though they are red as crimson, they shall be like wool."
—Isaiah 1:18

TANK. BLITZ. JOHANN. I don't know if those are their real names. In fact, I am sure they are not. They are simply the names I have given them. Tank, Blitz, and Johann are three dogs that greet me when I run my favorite trail here in Germany. Every time I run this particular trail I run past the fenced-in yard that imprisons them. When they run up to the fence and bark at me, I enjoy giving them a quick and friendly "Guten Morgen." One day as I was running, I was wondering what it was they would be saying to me if I could translate their barks. "If you keep running that slowly, you won't make it back by sunset!" is what I thought I heard Tank say. Blitz is a little more kind, commenting on my form. "Good power up the hill. Open your stride, and let your legs carry you." Johann is the quietest, yet most profound. One day I swear I heard him say, "I'm jealous. Enjoy the trail, enjoy your freedom."

I am free. I am able to run wherever I want, for however long I want (within physical limitations). The dogs bark at me because they are fenced in. They are restricted. They have physical limitations as to where they can go. Through observing their bondage, I have greater appreciation for my freedom to run. In thinking through the course of a marathon, I find Mile 4 to be one of freedom.

Slowly but surely the crowd of runners that created a restricting box is dissipating and thinning out. In the same manner, the weight of the jitters and nervousness felt at the starting line has been shed. The newly-found space and fallen weight leave me feeling light and free. I have found room to maneuver and am now in a nice methodical rhythm. I am free and it is a glorious feeling. All the stresses from the morning—what to eat, when to eat, where to park, how to find the starting line, etc.—are no longer issues. I am running the race and I am free.

As I witnessed Tank, Blitz, and Johann restricted and fenced in, I valued my freedom more. Seeing their bondage gave me a better appreciation for the freedom I have in Jesus Christ. The following story from an adventure I embarked upon a few years ago illustrates this point.

In the summer of 2006 I teamed with two other guys for the adventure of a lifetime. We loaded up about fifty pounds of gear on our road bicycles in Kennebunk, Maine, and spent the next thirty-two days peddling our way down to Jacksonville, Florida. Over the course of our trip we ventured in and out of thirteen states, and slept in motels, campsites, friends' houses and, when necessary, a few hundred yards off the road and into the woods out of sight. We were seeking an adventure, but our vision was much bigger than that. Our trip had a mission: to tell people about the hope that is only found in Jesus Christ. We entitled our journey "The Ride for His Glory," and our tag phrase was "Hope to the Hopeless." Our desire was to engage in conversation with as many people as we could, hoping they would ask us where we were going and why. That was our window to speak of our hope. It was certainly an adventure to be traveling this distance, yet if we were simply riding for the sake of a thrill ride, we were wasting our time, effort, and energy.

    Along the way I felt as though my eyes were opened to some of the hopeless people along the way. When I went to sleep at night, my mind would play a slideshow of all the hopeless people I had seen. There was one woman just outside of Boston who engaged us in conversation and left me with a broken heart. With feet full of sores and blisters, she was unable to walk to any destination greater than a few blocks. Without any family or friends in the area, the closest place of refuge for her was the local liquor store. Her daily trip to the store provided her with a false sense of hope and security. For the next few nights I struggled to fall asleep as I could not seem to get her off my mind.

    Our adventure continued, as did the number of hopeless people I saw. This was particularly evident and vivid in Washington, D.C. By God's providence we crossed paths with George, a man who shared his life story with us. His story was devastating to hear. Everything seemed to be going well for him until the death of his mother took his entire family by surprise. He flew home for the funeral, for which he used his entire life savings to pay, hoping to be reimbursed by his brother. Soon after the funeral, his brother, rather than repay him, took every remaining penny he had. Soon thereafter his wife walked out on him, his employer let him go, and his house was taken. In just a few months he had buried his mother; was betrayed by a brother; lost his family, job and home; and succumbed to hopelessness. We shared the evening together with George, enjoyed a burger together at McDonald's, prayed with him, and left trusting God to change his life. I don't know whether we actually impacted his life, but I do know his story changed mine.

After that night, I saw George and others in my dreams. Our trip was not one of ease, and every night's sleep was precious. Although I was physically exhausted, I was unable to easily fall asleep. My mind was failing to allow my body to wind down. If you have ever seen the play or a movie version of Charles Dickens' *A Christmas Carol*, you may remember Jacob Marley, the character who appeared to Ebenezer Scrooge. He looks scraggly, pale, and covered in chains. Weighed down by his chains, his back slumps, causing him to maintain an almost constant stare at the ground. Even today, *A Christmas Carol is* one of my favorite plays to watch. Yet without fail the presence of Mr. Marley startles me. In the same way, you would expect me to anticipate the barking of Tank, Blitz, and Johann, and you would expect me to be prepared for Jacob's arrival on stage; yet I am never quite prepared.

After that night in Washington, I continued to see George and others dressed in chains like Mr. Marley when falling asleep. The backdrop was pitch black, yet a small light shone on the individuals, revealing faces and eyes covered in hopelessness. Nothing I could say, and nothing I could do, could release them from their chains. The sights and sounds terrified me. I wish I could say the nightmares went away after a few nights, but they did not. I did not know what to do or how to change or stop the nightmares. I did not know why this was happening, but God did.

Shortly after our bike trip ended, I began my summer job as a junior high camp counselor. To some, thirty-two days on a bike followed by five weeks of working with junior high students sounds like torture, but for me it made for a phenomenal summer.

During my first week of camp, I found myself in charge of the afternoon sports activities. Inclement weather forced us into

FREEDOM

the gym one day, which left dodge ball as a perfect option. As the games continued, I sat in the bleachers, which also served as the jail for those who had been knocked out of the game. We played a few games and were nearing the end of our time. A quick glance at the clock informed me that if the current game ended too soon, we would not have enough time to play a whole new game; yet it would leave us with too much time to easily waste. Enough time to do something, but not enough time to really do much of anything. A horrible place to be in with a gym full of antsy and hyper kids. So I declared a "jailbreak" to allow all the imprisoned kids back into the game. As I did, I will never forget what happened.

The kids came running out, yelling, celebrating, screaming, "We're free! We're free! We are back in the game!" They were high-fiving, jumping up and down, rejoicing in their new-found freedom. I was a little taken back, wanting to tell them, "It's only a game. It's not that big of a deal." But in that moment, I could almost feel Jacob Marley nearby. But this time it was no longer someone from the bike trip. It was no longer somebody whose eyes were filled with utter hopelessness. This time it was as if Jesus were covered in chains. At first I didn't like what I saw. It was scary, hard to see, and hard to grasp. The figure of Marley, and the sounds of the chains, had been something that startled and scared me. It was not what I wanted to associate my Savior with. Yet as he stretched out his arms and made the shape of a cross, the chains fell to the ground and made the most exhilarating thud as they fell. The thud echoed in the gym and pounded my heart. As they fell, I once again heard the kids screaming, "We are free! We are back in the game!"

I never could have predicted all of those events. Yet it happened. I would have never guessed that in my summer as a camp counselor the kids would teach me more than I could ever hope to teach them. But they did. I could not foresee the game of dodge ball impacting me in such a huge way. But it did.

It is hard to grasp how God's only Son would come to Earth to take the punishment of my sin. But He did. It is amazing that he who was without sin would come and become sin so that I, a depraved sinner, through his blood may be seen as blameless and pure. Yet his love *is* that amazing. That the innocent would willingly take the place of the guilty seems outrageous. But that's exactly what happened. Now I, who cannot pay the debt through my own actions, am free through the actions of the Holy One. I have been freed from the eternal punishment of sin through the blood of Christ that was shed on the Cross.

Seeing those kids jump up and down and rejoicing illustrated the freedom we have in Christ. We are free from all commendation through the blood of Jesus. Our debt has been paid and we are free. In a world that offers little to rejoice in, Jesus offers hope. Without him we are hopeless. Yet, because of him, we have hope. The weight of our sinful chains was taken off of our shoulders and put on Jesus'. We are forgiven and we are set free from the bondage of sin.

Run and enjoy your freedom. Enjoy the feeling of not being fenced in and not having any limitations, of being able to run where you want. May you run the race of life enjoying the freedom that comes from the blood of Jesus that was shed on the cross. He has paid the price so that you may be free from sin.

Father, we thank you for sending your Son, Jesus, to Earth to pay the debt we cannot pay. Thank you for his willingness to endure the cross, knowing the joy that was before him. Jesus, your blood has given us freedom. May we run in such a way that reflects this freedom. Thank you, Lord, for using your little children to change lives. It is in your name we pray. Amen.

MILE 5
GOALS

"If you don't know where you're going,
you will end up somewhere else."
—Yogi Berra

"Goals are the fuel in the fiery furnace of achievement."
—Brian Tracy

"Though you have not seen him, you love him, and even though you do not see him now, you believe in him and are filled with an inexpressible glorious joy, for you are receiving the goal of your faith, the salvation of your souls."
—1 Peter 8-9

I AM VERY thankful for the earthly father with whom God provided me. There are so many ways in which he shaped and helped me develop into the man of God I have become, and he continues to do so. Every step of the way he was there encouraging me, challenging me, and loving me.

Growing up, whenever I was about to begin a clear chapter of life, my dad would make me sit down and write out my goals. At the start of a school year, at the start of a sports season, and at the start of a new relationship, I was encouraged to write out goals. A few months later, they were pulled out and my progress (or lack thereof) was evaluated. My dad never handled this in an authoritarian way, but always with love and guidance. My dad wanted me to have goals, see myself accomplish them, and continually push myself. Writing out my goals gave me direction. I had to assess where I currently was, and then I had to think about where I wanted to go. Not only that, but it helped me think about how I was going to go about getting there. Taking the time to create some goals provides direction, encouragement, and motivation.

As you approach Mile 5, the reality of what you are up against has set in. For many, five miles is a decent midweek mileage run. That distance was not too bad during a training run, yet when you hit Mile 5 in a marathon, you slowly realize that you are not even one-fifth of the way through the race.

For me, it is important to break things down into bite-sized chunks. Five miles is a decent size, but when I hit Mile 5, it is hard to believe that I have to do that distance five more times, and I *still* won't be done. At that point in the race, it is extremely important to know why you are running and to know what your goals are. If you don't know where you are going, it is virtually impossible to get there.

There are plenty of reasons why people decide to run a marathon. Perhaps your goal is to prove yourself capable of running 26.2 miles. Upon telling your friends you were planning on running a marathon you were not greeted with encouragement and enthusiasm, rather a mocking laugh. Now you need to prove to your friends that you can do it. Maybe you want to test yourself. 5k (3.1 miles) and 10k (6.2 miles) races no longer prove to be challenging distances, and

GOALS

therefore the next step is 42k (26.2 miles). Some have the goal of going out and raising money for a specific cause. It is thrilling and amazing to see people raise money in connection with their races. Also, there are those who run because they are competitive and need an event in which to compete.

Whatever your goals are, you need to know why you are running a marathon. You need to sit down and write out your goals for your race. What are your training goals? What is your target for a finishing time? Not only this, but it would be wise to come up with a few different goals for the actual race. Regardless of how much or little time I have spent training, one of my goals while running a marathon will always be to finish. From this I can then determine what my dream goal will be, as well as my satisfactory goal. Establishing these goals prior to the race will encourage and motivate me during my training. Reminding myself of these goals while on the fifth mile will continue to give me the encouragement and motivation I need.

Amidst the multitude of reasons to run, one I enjoy the most is the fellowship of running with another person. Here is a quick story illustrating the point.

Living overseas has meant that the time I get to spend with family and friends is severely limited. Trips back to the States are infrequent, and even when they do happen, it is not guaranteed that I will be in the same geographic location as my closest friends. One summer I returned for a few weeks and was able to do a little whirlwind tour that enabled me to see a few friends. Unfortunately, schedules did not grant me much time with everyone. In fact, with one of my closest friends, Jack, we were only able to find a ninety-minute window of time in which we were both free. With only ninety minutes, you would think a cup of coffee, sitting at a table and talking would be the most beneficial use of our time, right? Wrong. For the majority of that time Jack and I took off on a ten-mile run together. We didn't run at a comfortable pace where we could talk the whole time; we pushed each other. The bond and fellowship we shared while running was greater than what we could have experienced over a cup of coffee. Running, competing, and pushing one another are what we had always done, and this was not about to change simply because we only had ninety minutes to share. At one point while running Jack started laughing, looked at me, and said, "I can hear someone asking me, 'Did you get the opportunity to see Tommy this summer?' I would respond and say, 'Yes,' but when they asked, 'What did you guys do? Did you talk a lot? Share a bunch of stories? Get caught up on life?' My response will be, 'No. We went for a ten-mile run! But no words were necessary, just running with one another again allowed for us to share more with each other than words could.'" Jack was exactly right with that comment. We did not need to spend that time lost in conversation. Being lost in the woods on a run was what we needed. There is such a unique bond that is formed when you partner with someone and run alongside him, and perhaps this is your goal for running a marathon.

To be honest, the greatest thing about my ten-mile run with Jack was not so much the time we spent together, but his willingness to help me accomplish my goal. Jack was aware that I was training for a marathon and in every way he could, Jack made it his goal to ensure that I accomplished mine. He sent emails to check up on my progress. He called to deliver a pep talk when I was discouraged. He ran with me in some pretty hot and miserable weather to join the struggle with me. His goal was to help me accomplish my goal.

In reading through Peter's first epistle, we see his goal is to help his brothers and sisters in Christ achieve their goal in becoming more transformed into the image of Jesus Christ. Aware of their current trials, Peter encourages them to persevere in their pursuit of holiness. As they live in a society full of sin and evil, he strengthens them to live in such a way that their good deeds are seen and God is given the glory. Knowledgeable of possible disunity, he inspires them to be sympathetic, like-minded, and loving. Peter's goal was to help his brothers and sisters accomplish their goal.

Within the very first words of his letter, Peter identified his audience as God's elect. From the research that has been done since the penning of Peter's letter, we have learned that he was writing to churches suffering persecution. With this in mind, Peter wanted them to remember to whom they belonged. A few sentences later,

GOALS

in the third verse, he once again reminded the people that they belong to Jesus, and that Jesus had given them new birth and a living hope. Once again, in the ninth verse of the second chapter, Peter painted a picture of whose they are "... a chosen people, a royal priesthood, a royal nation, a people belonging to God...."[13]

Peter recognized the situation these people were in, and he knew they needed a gentle reminder of their oneness with Christ. The difficulties they were facing were real. The pain, both physical and emotional, was excruciating. Yet a reminder of whom they belonged to was enough to provide them the encouragement, excitement, and passion they needed so that they could declare the praises of the one who called them out of darkness and into light.[14]

Peter knew they needed this reminder because he was aware of their present circumstances, and it was his aim to help them triumph. Peter encouraged his friends in the first six verses of his first letter to them, where he recognized their current struggles. He reiterated this point again in the seventeenth verse of the fourth chapter, as he once again identified with the audience. Interestingly, in both of these instances, Peter encouraged them to rejoice during their trials. Peter challenged them to make it a goal of theirs to take delight in the Lord, and to be glad of their situation.

Lastly, Peter laid before the churches the goal to recognize who they were, and who they are now, after being saved by the blood of Christ. This is first seen in chapter one, verse fourteen, where he stated, "As obedient children, do not conform to the evil desires you had when you lived in ignorance." Peter was attempting to paint a picture for his friends. Throughout the letter he was saying, "This is who you were and when you were living in sin you acted according to the sinful ways of the world. But now, you are a new creation and you are not who you once were."

Some may have turned from their wicked ways and felt it was only right to associate with those who shared their beliefs. Yet Peter also urged them to "Live such good lives among the pagans that, though they accuse you of doing wrong, they may see your good deeds and glorify God on the day he visits us."[15] This could only happen if they were still rubbing shoulders with the pagans. Peter was not encouraging them to isolate themselves from the rest of society. Rather, he encouraged them to recognize who they were compared to who they had become, and live in such a way that the pagans recognized the change.

If these straightforward words were not enough in the second chapter, Peter once again reiterated this point in the fourth chapter, where he said, "For you have spent enough time in the past doing what pagans chose to do ... they are surprised that you do not join them in their reckless, wild living, and they heap abuse on you."[16] Through the audience remembering their position in Christ, Peter said that those around them would take notice and recognize they were different.

Take the time and outline your personal goals for your race. Provide yourself with a target at which to aim. And as you sit down to write out your goals, spend some time and focus on the goals of those around you. What are the goals of your closest friends, the ones you can help them accomplish? What are the academic, social, spiritual, or athletic goals of your son or daughter that they need a parent to help them accomplish? What are the goals you have for your marriage that you and your spouse should discuss?

Peter was writing to a specific group of people who lived thousands of years ago. But his words are applicable to us as well. Peter was a prime example of a goal-minded individual. While I am certain he had goals for himself, his writings also reveal his goals for his friends.

Father, your goal is for us to be transformed more and more into the image of your Son, Jesus Christ. There will be bumps and bruises along the way. Our journey will be marked by trials we must persevere through: People surrounding us full of sin and evil intent, and disunity that can break hearts. In those moments and situations, Father, enable us to be Peters who seek others out and help them accomplish their goals. Amen.

MILE 6
COMPANIONSHIP

"Friendships born on the field of athletic strife are the
real gold of competition. Awards become corroded,
friends gather no dust."
—Jesse Owens

"The marathon is not really about the marathon,
it's about the shared struggle. And it's not only
the marathon, but the training."
—Bill Buffum

"Since they could not get him to Jesus because of the
crowd, they made an opening in the roof above Jesus,
and after digging through it, lowered the mat the
paralyzed man was lying on. When Jesus saw their faith,
he said to the paralytic, 'Son your sins are forgiven.'"
—Mark 2:4-5

*I*T HAS BEEN said that one of the greatest longings of the human heart is to know and be known. Even the most secluded and introverted person reading this, whether you want to admit it or not, has a longing for companionship. Everyone has this craving because our Creator instilled it in us. From the very beginning of mankind, God created Eve, for he knew that it was not good for Adam to be alone.[17] Adam was in need of someone who would be a suitable helper. God created us as creatures that need community and companionship.

Life is too difficult to make the journey alone. During the challenging times (as well as the good), we need people around us. We need friends and companions. We need those who will encourage us,[18] sharpen us,[19] spur us on,[20] correct us,[21] and hold us accountable. Going through life alone is a very difficult thing. Likewise, training for a marathon on your own can be very difficult.

As of the time of this writing, I have finished three marathons. For two of the three I trained by myself. Granted, every now and then I was able to convince someone to go along with me on a training run—whether they were joining me for a shorter run or riding a bike next to me while I ran. If you have someone who is biking alongside you, let him (or her) know that you realize it will be easy for him to ride at your running pace. Riding at Mile 10 will be easy. Riding at Mile 16 will be comparatively easy, even though you may be huffing and puffing. Inform the bike rider that any and all sarcastic comments about the ease of riding are NOT appreciated nor entertaining. Mom—please note.

It is not a coincidence that my fastest marathon time was the race in which I trained with someone. For two-thirds of our training, we were hundreds of miles apart and our target finish times differed by forty-five minutes. Despite this, there was something about the companionship that made the training and actual race easier. Following the same training plan meant that we were running the same distances, which allowed for there to be an understanding that did not take long to explain. Additionally, there was an unwritten code of accountability. If I chose to skip a training run, I was not only cheating myself, I was cutting corners on my running partner.

COMPANIONSHIP

Having a running companion not only creates accountability, but also it has a way of breaking down walls, allowing for unique bonds to be established. I do not know how and why this special bond occurs—maybe because when you run together you are pushing yourselves, you both go outside your comfort zones, and you are experiencing together the freedom first discovered in Mile 4. By letting your guards down you are able to connect and relate to your running partner(s). Things that might normally separate you (vocation, age, gender, etc.) lose their effect while running. It doesn't matter if one person is a CEO at a Fortune 500 company and the other is retired. The running trail has a way of leaving that all behind and equalizing everyone.

As you travel through the sixth mile, it helps to know that you are not alone. Perhaps that means knowing that a friend or family member is somewhere along the trail to cheer you on. Or you have a companion who is running stride for stride with you throughout the race. It may even be friends around the world who know of your endeavor and although not physically there, are still supporting you. Throughout Mile 6 you will find the longing for companionship.

There are plenty of biblical examples of companionship. Moses led, trained, and walked with Joshua until it was time to turn over his leadership role.[22] David and Jonathan were best friends. Jonathan was willing to give up the riches of the palace in order to protect the one he loved as himself.[23] Shadrach, Meshach, and Abednego were uprooted from their country, stood strong before a king, refused to nudge in their convictions, and worshiped God together.[24] As they worshiped together they literally walked through a fiery furnace side-by-side. Barnabas, whose name means "son of encouragement," was a companion to Paul on his missionary journeys.[25] My favorite example, however, is found in Mark 2.

The men who exhibit companionship in Mark 2 are not given names, so for the sake of the story I am going to name them Ross, Croce, Chris, and Manny. Typically, this story is approached by trying to understand Jesus' words and actions from healing physically and spiritually. However, I would like to focus on the handicapped man ("the paralytic") and his four friends (Ross, Croce, Chris, and Manny).

Society had shunned the paralytic as an outcast. He was despised and forgotten. Many assumed he or someone in his family had committed some terrible sin and therefore his lame body was his punishment. In spite of this, the man had four incredible friends. I pray that all of us have the vision and strength to be friends like these four.

The paralytic had virtually nothing to offer his friends. Imagine what life was like for this man. He was confined to a mat no bigger than three feet by six feet. Someone had to feed him, carry him, clothe him, and move him so he would not get bed sores. He had no prospects of surgery, rehab, or treatment. His whole life was spent on a mat. He did not contribute to society. In fact, he was a drain on society. He was unable to work and/or to obtain food by his own power. But he likely still had dreams. Dreams of one day walking, perhaps dreams of having a healthy body. Maybe even a family of his own.

In those days, associating with a paralytic was an abnormal and taboo thing to do. This fact apparently did not faze these four friends; they continually carried him where he needed to be and needed to go. I imagine they stood up for him when others mocked and scowled at him. When others walked by and ridiculed him, I bet his friends were there to protect him.

While some sneered, the friends carried. Some mocked; they stood up. Some scowled; they protected. They did all of these things knowing he had no way to repay them and nothing to offer them in return. What a beautiful picture of companionship. Our society could use a few more people like Ross, Croce, Chris, and Manny. Can you envision how our coworkers could be changed upon witnessing or even receiving this kind of friendship?

I could finish the story here and feel satisfied and content that those four have given us more than enough to ponder for a few weeks. Yet their story is not finished. A companion is one who is frequently in the company of someone else. I find it fascinating,

COMPANIONSHIP

challenging, and not one bit coincidental that these four men are in the presence of their friend when Jesus comes to their town.

When the four men found out Jesus was coming to town, they wanted to hear and see him. They no doubt had heard stories about him and about his teaching and healing power. They could not pass up the opportunity to see Jesus nor did they want their friend to miss out. So they said, "We will pick you up at nine o'clock," and they literally meant "pick you up." They carried him to Jesus. Who knows how far they had to walk, who knows how many hills they had to climb—but to these four men, it was all worth it in order to have their friend meet Jesus. Companions like Ross, Croce, Chris, and Manny will carry you to Jesus.

When they finally made it to the house where Jesus was, there was no room. The house was overflowing with people, none of whom were going to make way for a paralytic. All that work for a closed door. All that excitement, gone. Imagine the blow this was to the paralytic. The whole way there, he was telling his friends, "I want to hop on one foot when I get off this mat. I want to play duck-duck-goose with the little kids in our neighborhood. I want to enjoy some coffee that I purchased by being able to walk there *myself*. I want to be healed!"

Then the bomb drops as he sees a crowd so big the doors are overflowing. His tears of excitement and joy soon turn to tears of sadness. His dreams of being able to walk seem more lame and broken than his body. Now he just wants to be carried away, out of the big crowd, to avoid all the awkward stares and degrading comments. He wants to be away from people. He realizes that he is an outcast, disregarded by society. "It was a stupid thought anyway, let's just go home. I don't want to be here," the paralytic likely said. Full of embarrassment and disappointment, he wanted to disappear.

Yet his friends were not satisfied. His friends were not finished. They were not content. They came with a purpose to help their friend, and they were not leaving until they accomplished their mission. Companions like Ross, Croce, Chris, and Manny do not give up.

I imagine Manny, the engineer of the group, said, "If we can't get through the door, let's make our own! Buddy, you're going through the roof!"

So they started ripping away straw, sawing through wood, doing all they could to break open the roof. They created a hole big enough to fit their friend through. They attached him to some rope and lowered his mat, with him on it, down in front of Jesus and into the massive crowd.

Mark 2:5 states that "when Jesus saw **their** faith he said …" (emphasis added). Their faith was plural. It was more than just that of the paralytic. Jesus saw the faith of the paralytic AND his friends. Companions like Ross, Croce, Chris, and Manny will believe in you when others won't.

Imagine the silence and stunned faces as people in the house stared at the man on the mat coming through the roof. This was not an everyday occurrence. Jesus looked at the man and peered up at the hole in the roof with four heads poking through. He saw their smiles, he saw their joy, he saw their faith. And then he told the paralytic he was forgiven and granted him the first steps of his new life.

While you may not be crippled physically, the difficulties of this life may have confined you emotionally to a mat. Do you have a group of people that are carrying you on your mat? Are you surrounded by a group of friends from whom you do not hide? Are there those who know you well enough to know when you are hurting and weak? Do you have friends who hear the answer to the question, "How are you?" and can completely see through the masked lies of the half-hearted answer that everything is fine? It can be scary and intimidating to allow people to know you in such a way, but you will be thankful for those who will carry you when you hurt. Who carries you when you are on your mat?

You are now finishing Mile 6 of your race. You have run more than 20 percent of the course. Most likely you have been running for nearly an hour. It is my experience that right about now, you need a companion. The excitement from the starting line has worn off. The thick masses of crowds have thinned out and become sparse.

COMPANIONSHIP

The seeds of doubt start to whisper to you, "Are you really capable of continuing?" Hopefully you have companions around you. Yet, looking at Peter's example in Mile 5, we must also take the focus off of ourselves and look around us.

Who in your daily sphere of influence could use some companionship? Ask your heavenly Father to open your eyes and show you who you can carry today. Ask Jesus to show you the troubled souls around you that need your help. For in the same way that we need to be surrounded by such friends, we need to surround others. Do not let the day end without being someone who is willing and able to carry a mat for a friend.

***

Father, thank you for all you have given us. Thank you for the opportunities you present us with to be carried as well as to carry others. Please open our eyes so that we may see those around us who need encouragement. May we be open and willing to move when you open the doors for us. May those around us be changed as a result of the way in which we treat our friends. Amen.

MILE 7
LONELINESS

"Loneliness and the feeling of being unwanted is the most terrible poverty."
—Mother Teresa

"But Jesus often withdrew to lonely places and prayed."
—Luke 5:16

"About the ninth hour Jesus cried out in a loud voice, 'Eloi, Eloi lama sabachthani?' which means, 'My God, my God, why have you forsaken me.'"
—Matthew 27:46

THE FOLLOWING IS an excerpt taken from my running journal on March 11, 2011:

Day off

"I love Fridays. Well, my body loves Fridays, but for some insane reason, my mind causes me to feel lazy if I'm not out there running or doing something physical. My body needs the rest and I fully recognize that, which explains why I will not do anything today. However, for some strange reason my brain wants to go for a run. I suppose I have an emotional need to run. Maybe I'm addicted to it. I know that my heart is heavy and full of weight today. Part of my heart really wants to release tears. Something in my heart is really itching for the 'flood gates' to open. My mind knows that a run would allow me that opportunity. It may be sweat and not tears, but the moisture would do my heart good. Face it, TB! Don't run away. Run toward the battle. Believe the truth; let the lies of the devil pass you by. Be strong and courageous."

It may seem odd to have a chapter about loneliness immediately following a chapter about companionship, but my experience has been that Mile 7 of a race can be the loneliest mile in the marathon. The crowds have started to thin. Perhaps the weather is taking its toll, whether it be the heat, the rain, or the cold. Some in your running pack may start to drop out, realizing the task at hand is more than they can handle. Instead of running and constantly seeing fellow runners around you, as you look around you notice and feel as though you are alone.

Marathons find a unique way of paralleling the race of life. Waves of loneliness frequently follow phases of companionship. I do not know why that is. I am even less certain of how to change it.

LONELINESS

The definition of loneliness includes the concept of being companionless. Many of us deal with this issue, regardless of whether we want to admit it. If you have never felt alone, feel free to skip this chapter and move on to the next chapter. But if you have experienced loneliness, read on.

Loneliness is a common assailant to the human heart. It is also an emotion filled with a great paradox—many people continually feel alone, and yet they are not alone in feeling that way.

How does one accurately describe the pit in your stomach when you feel alone? How can mere words on paper express the hurt and heaviness that can overtake your heart? Most of us have felt it, yet we cannot fully describe it. I find that frustrating. Fear that others won't understand your hard-to-express emotions often leaves you secluded, quiet, unwilling to share, and alone.

There have been many runs on which I have gone out with a heavy heart. My goal may have been to simply work up a sweat and let my mind rest for a while. Without intending it, sometimes something strange happens on those runs and tears fall in larger quantities than sweat. This has happened to me more than once. One such run occurred in the late winter of 2011 in the trails tucked away in the hills of Germany's Black Forest.

For a moment I would like to go back to companionship. Barry was one of my closest companions, starting in college. Many would not have pegged the two of us to be close friends. We played together for four years on our college's soccer team, and the bond created within those white lines was priceless. To be honest, while practicing we did not like each other a whole lot. It was common for the two of us to get heated and shove one another around in the spirit of competition. We purposely set ourselves up on opposite teams in practice, knowing we would force each other to play our best. Yet as soon as we finished practice we were friends again, joking, laughing, hanging out. We were able to leave the competition on the field. Off the field, our friendship stretched over a variety of areas and enjoyed a rare depth.

Barry and I were both history majors, allowing us to share many classes together and giving our friendship another dynamic.

We spent many late nights together studying for tests and/or proofreading each other's papers. On the bus traveling to and from soccer games, we often engaged in history debates with one of us intentionally arguing an opposing point of view simply to generate a reaction and spark a debate. Our competitive natures would not allow us to back down, whether on the soccer field or in a "friendly" debate.

Above all, Barry and I shared a similar faith and a similar desire to grow in that faith. Without planning it, in between our junior and senior years we both participated in summer-long sports ministries. Barry's took him to Latin America while mine took me to Italy and England. Though thousands of miles apart and in countries that speak different languages, it felt as though we were working together, for we were ultimately on the same team, hoping to accomplish the same eternal goals.

In our post-collegiate occupations, we found ourselves filling similar roles, once again on the soccer field; this time not as players but as coaches. Barry lived in the United States while I was in Germany, yet we were both ecstatic to be coaching soccer. In our conversations about our teams, I felt as though few words were needed since the other understood. In fact, looking back that seems to be one of the greatest aspects of our friendship. Whether playing, serving, studying, worshiping, or coaching, we understood each other. That simple yet profound fact enabled us to form and sustain an amazing friendship.

Unfortunately, that friendship ended sooner than I wanted. One afternoon I received a phone call from a friend with news about Barry. I sat in silence, too shocked to say anything. Barry had passed away in a drowning accident. The state of shock remained for a few days as I continually tried to convince myself it hadn't actually happened, hoping I would get a phone call saying that they had misidentified the body. While sleeping I would dream as if the phone call had never happened. No matter how much I wished it had not happened, I could not change the facts. As the news continued to sink in, a wave of loneliness swept in and took my heart captive.

LONELINESS

I was thousands of miles away from my other close friends who also knew Barry. I was in Germany trying to process, trying to grieve, when the ones I desperately wanted to be with were on the other side of the world. Phone calls were made and emails were exchanged, yet nothing could fill the void. I wanted to have someone next to me who knew Barry, who knew the memories, who knew our relationship. It was a lonely time. I wish I could say I took a magic potion, uttered a magic prayer, and everything was fixed and I no longer felt lonely. But the loneliness remained for weeks. Many within my community in Germany stepped up upon hearing the news and were a tremendous blessing. I could not have faced that situation without the love and support of those friends. Yet the loneliness continued. I felt as though nobody could relate. I felt alone in my pain. Alone in my processing. Alone in my loneliness.

During this struggle, I was two-thirds through my training program for an upcoming marathon. I had already signed up, made the arrangements, and trained intensely. I knew I couldn't back out now (remember ... discipline), so I kept running. A week prior to that phone call, my mind was carefree while running, enjoying the sights and sounds. Spring was quickly coming and my runs were showing my continued increase in strength and stamina. Now, it seemed as though I could not stop replaying memories, could not stop thinking of his family, could not stop my heart from wanting to be a thousand miles from where it really was. It was spring around me, but in my heart it was dark, cold winter.

During the week following that phone call, my training called for an easy five-mile run. The week had produced little sleep and a lot of tears. I took off down one of my favorite running trails, hoping to be able to clear my mind. Less than halfway through my run, my pace unnaturally slowed down. My run had become a jog, then a speed-walk, then a walk, then a weak walk to the point where I could barely keep myself standing. Overcome with emotion, I stopped and started yelling to God. Then it turned into yelling *at* God. I was questioning why this had to happen, wondering why it had to happen when it happened. Among all the questions pouring from my heart that day, none seemed to echo more loudly than this one: "God why do I feel so alone in all of this? Can there be someone, anyone, to help me through this?"

As I planned out this chapter I found something very interesting and moving hidden in the fifth chapter of Luke's gospel. Within this segment of Jesus' life, he often retreated to lonely places to pray. There is comfort in knowing that the Son of God visited a place of loneliness. The place he went was solitary. He was without companions, he was isolated—all feelings we experience during life and during a marathon. At surface level, am I the only one who finds that a bit bizarre? Jesus was surrounded by people. They followed him wherever he went. They questioned him and sat for hours to listen to him teach. They marveled at his words and his power. But why did Jesus feel lonely?

Not only was Jesus lonely in the garden as he prayed, he experienced a wave of loneliness on the cross. Loneliness is not a strong enough word to describe his pain. He felt abandoned.

Max Lucado has been my favorite author for quite some time. I have read all of his books. With every turn of the page, I am enlightened, entertained, and challenged. These words from his book *No Wonder They Call Him the Savior* paint a picture of Jesus' loneliness while on the cross;

> The despair is darker than the sky. The two who have been with God for eternity, is now alone. The Christ, who was an expression of God, is abandoned. The trinity is dismantled. The Godhead is disjointed. The unity is dissolved. It is more than Jesus can take. He withstood the beatings and remained strong at the mock trials. He watched in silence as those he loved ran away. He did not retaliate when the insults were hurled nor did he scream when the nails pierced his wrists. But when God turned his head, that was more than he could handle. "My God!" the wail rises from parched lips. The holy heart is broken. The sinbearer screams as he wanders in the eternal wasteland. Out of the silent sky come the words screamed by all who walk in the desert of loneliness. "Why? Why did you abandon me?"

LONELINESS

I believe that Jesus experienced loneliness so that he would be able to empathize with us as we travel through our own personal waves of loneliness. Also, in Jesus' moments of loneliness, he went to the Father. Both are extremely worthwhile lessons.

Jesus went through a period of loneliness so that he could comfort us when we go through lonely times. The author of Hebrews wrote about this a few times. In the second chapter he writes:

> Since the children have flesh and blood he too shared in their humanity so that by his death he might destroy him who holds the power of death … for this reason he had to be made like his brothers in every way, in order that he might become a merciful and faithful high priest in service to God, and that he might make atonement for the sins of the people. Because he himself was tempted, he is able to help those who are being tempted.[26]

A few verses later the author pens these words:

> Therefore, since we have a great high priest who has gone through the heavens, Jesus the Son of God, let us hold firmly to the faith we profess. For we do not have a high priest who is unable to sympathize with our weaknesses, but we have one who has been tempted in every way, just as we are—yet was without sin. Let us then approach the throne of grace with confidence, so that we may receive mercy and find grace to help us in our time of need.[27]

The apostle Paul expanded on this in his second letter to the church at Corinth:

> Praise be to the God and Father of our Lord Jesus Christ, the Father of compassion and the God of all comfort, who comforts us in all our troubles, so that we can comfort those in any trouble with the comfort we ourselves have received from God. For just as the sufferings of Christ flow over into our lives, so also through Christ our comfort overflows.[28]

Jesus went through trials of all kinds so that he could comfort us when we go through similar trials. What a phenomenal God we serve! I doubt many of us would willingly go through periods of loneliness. Yet Jesus chose to go through them so that he can empathize with you and me. When you are going through a period of loneliness, God understands.

Later in the book of Luke, it was reported that Jesus again retreated to solitary places to pray.[29] In so doing Jesus provides us with a great example as well as great comfort.

In our times of loneliness, we must go to the Father. During the waves of loneliness we face, the devil sees an opportunity to kick us while we are down. He wants to throw salt in our wounds. When lonely, many of us feel an empty void and search for ways to fill that void. There are healthy ways to fill that emptiness, and there are also ways that will tear us down and cause damage. There are ways that will momentarily fill that void only to find out later the empty space is now bigger. However, Jesus provides us with the perfect example of what we are to do in such situations—pray and go to the Father. It sounds good on paper. It sounds easy to do. For some reason it isn't all that easy, which is why remembering Jesus' actions is so important. Remember those runs when tears fell faster and heavier than sweat? Those moments when words could not express your heart's pain? Times in which you felt nobody understood? At times like that, we must follow Jesus' example.

Jesus experienced loneliness while on earth, so that when you face your period(s) of loneliness, he can wrap his loving arms around you and welcome you to a heart that understands.

Jesus, thank you for the example you set. Thank you for showing the way and letting us know that in our times of loneliness we should go to the Father and pray. Also, Jesus,

LONELINESS

thank you for being willing to come to Earth and go through all that we went through. You did it to show us that you understand and that you can comfort us in our times of loneliness. Thank you for reminding us that we are not alone; you are there with us. Amen.

MILE 8
PERSISTENCE

"You have a choice. You can throw in the towel, or you
can use it to wipe the sweat off of your face."
—Gatorade advertisement

"When I heard these things, I sat down and wept.
For some days I mourned and fasted and
prayed before the God of heaven."
—Nehemiah 1:4

WHAT DO YOU do when things don't seem to go your way? What happens when a wave of loneliness beats you down? How do you respond? How does your mind and body react to one of the more difficult miles in a marathon? You persist. You keep going. You continue in your path, maintaining an attitude that is unrelenting and unwilling to break down. You must be bold. Daring. Fearless.

Mile 8 has been one where I felt as though I could catch my breath physically as well as mentally and emotionally. This stems from my ability to get through the loneliness of Mile 7. Seeing the signs for Mile 8 brings with it a revived spirit and a rejuvenated passion to continue.

Prior to each race, I create a game plan that breaks the marathon into three eight-mile segments. As I reach the start of the eighth mile, I am 5,280 feet away from completing the first segment. I recognize that eight does not go evenly into twenty-six, but breaking the race into three segments makes it easier mentally. By the time you reach the two leftover miles—Miles 25 and 26—it is pure adrenaline and determination that carry you to the finish line. But those ending miles are much farther down the road. The eighth mile is one of persistence; one that requires a mentality that is fixed on enduring difficulty and opposition.

While there is much to rejoice for having completed the first of three segments, the race is not over. In one breath, you may celebrate getting past a tough seventh mile, but in the next breath you must be willing to persist through the next mile. As soon as you celebrate a victory from Mile 7, the eighth mile is staring you down. No matter how hard you fight something, it seems to be pushing back with equal strength. Mile 8 starts to get to your mind and legs. The crowd has thinned, as has your energy. Dig deep. Keep going. Don't give in, and don't allow anyone or anything to break your will.

The Scriptures are saturated with examples of men and women who lived lives characterized by persistence. As I took some time to look at these lives, I realized there were more examples than I had originally thought. Then it hit me. Those who claim to be saved from their sins through the blood of Jesus Christ—who was crucified, buried, and rose from the dead—are in a constant battle. It is true that the war has been won. We know how the story ultimately ends. Jesus has defeated Satan. Those who call upon his name and place their trust and faith in him are invited into an eternal relationship with God. However, until Jesus comes again, or the Lord calls us home, we will find ourselves engaged in a battle. It is our heart's desire to deepen our personal relationship with Jesus, to learn more about him, to learn more from him, and to continually be shaped more into his image. The devil desires to take every action he can to prevent any of that from happening. But the Bible encourages and instructs us through stories of individuals who persisted through difficult situations. This persistence cannot and will not be evident if the individual solely relies on human strength.

As was stated earlier, our courage comes from Jesus. Our discipline and patience are virtues instilled in us through the Holy Spirit. Our freedom comes solely as a result of the work Christ did on the cross; it has nothing to do with our own human efforts. In the same way, the ability to continue persistently comes from God. He alone is our source of strength, our fountain of energy. God is faithful and true. He is the same yesterday, today, and forever. Therefore, as we gaze back at the lives of our brothers and sisters in faith, we can see their failures and triumphs and recognize that the same strength they received from God is still available to us today.

In the beginning stages of planning this book, I first assigned one word to each mile. Following that I wrote down different biblical characters I felt served as good models of that particular word. In mapping out this chapter my mind quickly thought of Moses, and I penned him in. After all, Egypt was the place of one of his greatest mistakes, when he took the life of an Egyptian. He was led into exile and had forty years to think through his actions. Following these years of learning and perhaps loneliness, he was led back to the exact country of his great mistake. In returning he faced a hostile nation in the Egyptians *and* the Hebrews. Stubborn does not even begin to explain the heart of the Pharaoh. After multiple visits, and a spirit of persistence, God used Moses to soften the heart of Pharaoh and allowed the Hebrews to leave Egypt. Moses' persistence led to deliverance. Choosing Moses seemed simple, logical, and obvious.

I began researching different passages and different commentaries on Moses. I stumbled across a parable from Luke 5 where Jesus encouraged his followers to be persistent in prayer by sharing a story of a man whose friend came to his house in the middle of the night. In an attempt to display proper etiquette and be a good friend, the host searched for a way to feed his friend. Unable to do so through his own kitchen, he ventured to his neighbor's house and woke him. The tired and stubborn neighbor refused to lend a helping hand at first. Yet the host persisted. He knocked a second time, and knocked louder and louder, asking until he had what he needed. His persistence and unwillingness to give in allowed him to be a blessing to a friend in need.

I began to wonder if this parable would be a better springboard for persistence. First of all, it comes directly from the lips of Jesus, which is a pretty reliable source. Secondly, it deals with persistence in prayer which is something we could all use more of. I sadly left Moses back in Egypt and decided to research persistent prayers, which led me to Nehemiah.

We find Nehemiah tucked away in the sometimes overlooked pages of the Old Testament. Within his story, we witness a man whose spirit, through God's strength and guidance, was committed to persist in his task. Nehemiah proved to be a man with a vision and an unrelenting spirit. He faced various forms of opposition yet would not allow those obstacles to break him down and erode his focus. The verbal slander and ridicule hurled at him could not break his effort. The mockery of his enemies and false reports about him, directed with the intent to ruin his reputation, failed to discourage this man of persistent tenacity. Having failed with the first two attempts, his enemies threw a final arrow of destruction at him—a threat on his life. Even this could not derail Nehemiah's unrelenting spirit.

PERSISTENCE

I love where we first find Nehemiah. He was not out running his mouth with these great plans he had. He was not sitting in self-pity as a hostage in a foreign country. He was on his knees communicating with God. Recognize where Nehemiah's attitude of persistence found its roots—in God and God alone. After hearing the news of Jerusalem's walls falling, his next days were spent fasting, weeping, and praying. Through these exercises Nehemiah walked away more encouraged and more full of an unrelenting heart. Do fasting, weeping, and praying automatically translate to a spirit of persistence? No. But if we desire to accomplish the things of God, we need to remain in tune with him. This is a great time to be reminded of Jesus' words:

> I am the vine; you are the branches. If a man remains in me and I in him, he will bear much fruit; apart from me you can do nothing. If anyone does not remain in me, he is like a branch that is thrown away and withers; such branches are picked up, thrown into the fire and burned. If you remain in me and my words remain in you, ask whatever you wish, and it will be given you.[30]

Through this story we can learn more about Nehemiah's heart, as well as the heart of God. We will later see that Nehemiah was persistent when dealing with the opposition around him. But as we note in 1:6, Nehemiah was persistent with God. In his pleading with God, he revealed that he had been praying day and night. That is persistence at its finest. In verses eight and nine Nehemiah is saying, in essence, "God, this is what you said you would do if your people were unfaithful. We were, and you did exactly what you said you would do. But you also said if they repented, you would gather them, regardless of how far they were scattered and how much they messed up. Here I am repenting. Hold up your end of the bargain." Thus we get to see a part of God's character: his faithfulness.

As the story continues Nehemiah was not yet at the point when he could start building the wall. He must first obtain permission from the king prior to leaving. I love how the story unfolds in the opening verses of the second chapter. The king asked Nehemiah a direct question and without hesitating Nehemiah prayed to God, searching for the right words to use.

Beyond his continual integrity of persistent prayer, Nehemiah was a highlight reel for self-control. As we can clearly see from the first chapter, he was distraught with the condition of the wall and his people. Nehemiah was passionate and emotional about the project he was about to present to the king.

How often, in our moments of passion and high emotion, do we let words slip off our tongue that should have been contained? How often do we seize an opening in a conversation, speaking words that carry weight and magnitude we cannot begin to comprehend? We could all use more self-control, especially when it comes to our tongue. The book of James is full of words of caution regarding the tongue and its power. How wonderful to see a great example in Nehemiah of an individual who controlled his tongue. What was his secret? Prior to opening his mouth, he prayed to God. Nehemiah was persistently in conversation with God.

Nehemiah also gave us another golden nugget of truth from his conversation with the king—acknowledgement and proper praise to the one who deserved it. The king granted Nehemiah's request, and Nehemiah came back, telling his friends, "I talked with the king and he loved what I said. He was so impressed with my presentation. I did my research and knew exactly how to approach him and how to hit his sweet spot. I did such a good job speaking to him, and I convinced him to let us go ahead with the project. I did a great job!" Wrong. Read Nehemiah 2:8 again: "… and because the gracious hand of my God was upon me, the king granted my requests." Nehemiah recognized that he did nothing; it was God's hand that did everything. Nehemiah recognized the fact that if the wall was going to be rebuilt it would only come to completion if God was involved in every step. When the pieces started to fall into place, he was quick to jump out of the spotlight and make sure everyone knew it was God's hand that had set everything in motion. Since God's hand was involved in the project, Nehemiah was able to withstand the attacks that would soon come his way.

PERSISTENCE

    As Nehemiah and his crew began rebuilding the wall, they immediately faced opposition. Sanballat, Tobiah, and Geshem, three men adamantly opposed to Nehemiah, his people, and especially his God, formed an alliance against Nehemiah hoping to break his will and derail his project. Nehemiah 2:19-20 tells us that they mocked and ridiculed the builders. The dictionary defines "ridicule" as "speech or action intended to cause contemptuous laughter at a person or thing." Mockery is seen as actions that ridicule. Sanballat, Tobiah, and Geshem were trying to break Nehemiah's will. They were trying to irk him and convince him to throw in the towel and give up.

    These three continued their insults as they mocked the size of the wall and the progress the Israelites had made. It appears as though these three were there watching as the project started, and as progress was made, they were still standing there hurling insults. Nehemiah was not the only persistent character within this story. His adversaries were persistent in their hope to break his will.

    If Nehemiah had not faced enough already, there was another trial coming his way that he had to endure and overcome—the possibility of an attack on his life and the life of all those working on the wall. At this point we should not be surprised that our three stooges are at the root of this squabble. In Nehemiah 4:8 we see a glimpse of their plan as "they all plotted together to come and fight against Jerusalem and stir up trouble against it."

    Once again we see a man persistent in prayer when we see Nehemiah's immediate reaction: "But we prayed to our God and posted a guard day and night to meet this threat." He recognized the situation and took practical and sound action to ensure his safety and, more important to him, the safety of those around him. They split their workforce. Half were stationed as guards ready to fight in an instant, and the other half continued to build. They, too, were prepared for anything as "those who carried materials did their work with one hand and held a weapon in the other."[31] Nehemiah and his workers were prepared. They were ready for an attack at any hour of the day, from any direction. As part of their preparation, they had the necessary tools needed to ward off any attack. How prepared are you for any attacks that may come your way?

Not satisfied with their inability to break Nehemiah's will or take his life, the three adversaries decided to take it one step further as they attempted to break his reputation. Again, it is intriguing that Sanballat, Tobiah, and Geshem were extremely persistent in their attempt to bring down Nehemiah and his project. They sent a message claiming they simply wanted to have a chat while enjoying some coffee (OK, I added the coffee part) when in reality they were planning to physically harm him. After receiving a "thanks, but no thanks" from Nehemiah, they sent the invitation one more time. Once again Nehemiah declined. In all, this exchange happened four times. Four separate times these three continued their effort to derail Nehemiah. Finally, after the fourth failed effort, they altered their approach—they spread rumors and attempted to ruin his reputation by attacking his character. They claimed that Nehemiah was working on the walls so that he could provide himself with a platform to become king.

Nehemiah was selfless, yet they claimed he was selfish. Nehemiah was doing this for The King, yet they claimed he wanted to be king. Nehemiah was humble, and they claimed he was full of pride. He exerted time, energy, and resources to help the poor. They insisted he only wanted to help himself.

Have you ever had your character challenged? Has your integrity ever been under scrutiny? It is one thing if there is just cause for the accusations, yet when there is no justifiable reason, the accusations jump to a whole new level. It is not an enjoyable place to be. When those around you are talking *about* you, but not talking *to* you. When they are shouting things they heard whispered second-, third-, or fourth-hand. With each person the information gets passed to, the amount of truth dwindles, yet somehow the lies prevail.

If you find yourself in such a situation, bear in mind two truths that will hopefully carry you through your trial. Following the accusations of the three stooges, Nehemiah stood up and gave them a short reply, informing them of their incorrect information, and then he prayed. As much as I admire Nehemiah for his visible persistence in all that was required of him to rebuild the walls, I am more impressed with his persistence in prayer. When he needed guidance, he prayed. When he sought answers, he prayed. When things were going well, he prayed. When things were going against him, he prayed. When he was in conversation with the king, and there was a slight momentary pause, he stopped to pray. Picking up from the example left by Nehemiah, if you find yourself in a situation in which your reputation is in question, be a man or woman of prayer.

And as you pray to the God of the universe, I encourage you to pray for those who are at the root of your troubles. As you pray for them, be open and willing to allow your heart to change. Few could blame you for being angry with those who are trying to ruin your reputation. Most would not give a second thought if you wrote off those who are trying to break your will. Still, I urge you to pray for them. While doing so, pray that God would change your heart and your attitude toward them. There is something amazing about praying for your enemies as your heart releases the pain and hatred and welcomes compassion, kindness, and grace. Though they are creating difficulty for you, we are not excused from loving them. Whether we want to believe it or not, Christ went to the cross to die for their sins just as much as he went to the cross to die for your sins.

Nehemiah provides us with another—the ability to distinguish and separate the voice of truth from the lies. Prayer is not simply a one-way conversation. As we talk to God, he desires to respond and talk back, albeit not necessarily in an audible voice. As we communicate with God, we will be able to better hear his voice and his truth. In a society consumed with noise, we must learn how to block out all the lies and hear God's truth. No doubt there were nights while the wall was being built that Nehemiah went to the Lord disheartened and discouraged. Perhaps frustrated by the rumors spreading around him, he was able to be reassured of who he was in God's eyes. In the same way, when there are all sorts of lies flying around you, stay close to God and be in tune with what he is saying. When you are listening closely to the voice of truth, you will not be dismayed, for he is with you, promising never to leave you nor forsake you.

Nehemiah is a phenomenal example of one who persists through difficulty. Nehemiah was a man who endured everything tenaciously, even when his life was threatened. All of this was accomplished by obtaining a spirit of persistence. Nehemiah's unrelenting spirit ignited a fire in his soul. It formed the steel in his backbone that carried him through ridicule, mockery, and rejection. Like Nehemiah, our persistence must not be half-hearted or lukewarm. It must be bold. Daring. Fearless.

May your eighth mile be one of persistence.

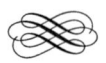

Father, thank you for your Word and the way in which it is filled with individuals who have modeled lives of persistence. You never told us that following you was going to be easy, in fact you were straightforward with saying it would be difficult. Yet you have not left us hanging out to dry. You have promised to never leave us nor forsake us, and you have proven yourself faithful countless times throughout history. Thank you for sending your Son, Jesus, who endured the cross to pay the payment for our sins, giving us the ultimate example. May you grant us mercy, grace, patience, and persistence as we are continually formed more and more into the image of your Son. Amen.

MILE 9
EXCITEMENT

"Relax. Take a deep breath. God is in control.
Have fun. Smile."
—My Dad

"You have to wonder at times what you're doing out
there. Over the years, I've given myself a thousand
reasons to keep running, but it always comes back to
where it started. It comes down to self-satisfaction
and a sense of achievement."
—Steve Prefontaine

"Be still and know that I am God; I will be exalted among
the nations, I will be exalted in all the earth."
—Psalm 46:10

SHORTLY AFTER FINISHING the rough draft for the previous chapter, I crawled into bed and tried to fall asleep. As much as I wanted to sleep, I couldn't help but think about the next chapter. My mind pondered the previous two chapters and looked ahead to the next few. In looking back, I felt as though the previous two chapters carried a lot of weight. They were definitely enjoyable to write, and I put my heart on paper, but they still seemed a bit heavy. Then I looked at my notes and saw the next chapter I planned to write was about excitement. I was relieved. For the past two chapters, we have trudged through some deep and heavy material—which I honestly think is representative of those miles within a marathon. As I fell asleep, I reminded myself, "Marathons are fun. Running is enjoyable. I love to run." Perhaps during Miles 7 and 8 you did not feel this, but it is my hope that by Mile 9 you have once again regained some of the initial excitement. Perhaps some of the energy that convinced you to run a marathon in the first place has once again surfaced.

Initially my vision was to write and walk through the marathon with you. But I realize very few of you will carry this book with you while running the actual race. In fact, nobody will do that. But if there is someone out there who thinks it would be funny to do so, please take a picture of it and send it to me!

Knowing perhaps you are reading this while training for a marathon, I realize there may be times within your training when you have lost excitement. The thrill of waking up early to run has lost its joy and the new joy is slapping the snooze button three times and staying in bed. The idea of a long run on the weekend brings thoughts of horror when you envision everything else on your schedule. Perhaps the thrill of waking up early and doing your devotions has lost its luster. The excitement to talk to your coworker about your faith has shrunk. You once prayed for an opening in a conversation to share your faith. Now you are praying the topic of faith never comes up in conversation. The past two miles were difficult, but do not allow that to define your next mile. The last few days, weeks, or months may have been difficult in regards to your relationship with God; do not allow that to define your next day.

EXCITEMENT

My life has had many ups and downs. Twists and turns have caused many bumps and bruises. Through different scenarios, I have found myself calling home stressed out, discouraged, and hurt. Most often I made that phone call because I wanted sympathy. My mind wanted other people to feel bad for me. Thankfully, my dad was able to recognize the difference between what my head wanted and what my soul needed. When I would make that phone call, he would get on the phone, and after a few words, my heart would be full of excitement once again. His words were simple yet profound, "Relax. Take a deep breath. God is in control. Have fun. Smile." His first words caused me to stop and be silent. After doing that, I was able to be reminded of the greatest truth—God is in control. Stop for a moment and allow that truth to make its way from your head down to your heart. God is in control.

Once I paused and allowed that truth to permeate my heart, an overwhelming sense of peace would overcome me. I smiled and got excited because the God of the universe loves me, cares for me, and is in control of all things. It did not mean circumstances would be easy. But I felt safe in His arms. That is exciting.

For those who may have lost the excitement of running, here is some homework. Take some time to answer the question, "Why do I run?" Pull out a pen and paper and write down the reasons you run. I imagine there is not anyone or anything forcing you to run, so there must be a reason. Why do you run?

After completing the marathon I mentioned in chapter seven, I was discouraged and beat down. While I had learned some invaluable lessons that day, I was still disappointed with my performance on the course. In the days that followed, I found it difficult to muster up the energy and excitement to lace up my shoes and go on a run. During this time my college soccer coach, who has been a running mentor to me, gave me the same homework I laid out in the paragraph above. He did not require I show it to him or anyone else, but said that I owed it to myself to sit down and honestly and truthfully answer the question. Doing so would help me determine my attitude and whether I should continue to pursue running marathons. Below are some segments from what I wrote:

… Why do I run? What is it that makes me want to go out in all kinds of weather and do something that will exhaust my body, tax my mind, and take up time? Simple answer: because I love it. I love to run. I love the feeling of getting out there and having nothing else to do, nowhere else to be, nobody breathing down your neck telling you what to do. When I run, I feel free. I am free to be myself, free to go where I want to go. Free to go as fast as I want, or as slow as I want …

… I remember the first few times I was old enough and strong enough to go on a run with my dad. That was a special thing, and something I will always remember. Running stride for stride next to your dad, next to your role model, your mentor, is something that is precious. It didn't matter how slow we were going, or what distance we covered, I was running with my dad, and that was enough …

… Spiritually, running provides me with a time of peace and quiet. Many times my runs and my thoughts are extended periods of prayer. A time where I can converse back and forth with God; where we can be alone, where we can talk and not be distracted. Sometimes I even listen to sermons while running, just because I'm in the mood to listen to something. It is not uncommon for me to go out on a run and pray, asking God, "Who needs encouragement right now? Who around me could use a note? An email? An encouraging conversation?" While running, I let those closest to me run through my mind until God points to a few of them, and tells me to do my best to bless them …

… I want to push myself—all the time, in all areas of my life. I don't want to be content and feel as though I have "arrived." I am learning more and more every day how far I still have to go in many areas of my life, running being one of many. One of the things I hate the most is being in a position where I am not pushed. In running I can always push myself, I am in control of that and can be in charge of how hard I push …

… When I write these thoughts, I come back to the conclusion that I absolutely love running. I love the feeling, I love the

EXCITEMENT

satisfaction, I love the adrenaline, I love the companionship, I love the time it gives me …

As a result of my answering the question, "Why do you run?" I came back to a crucial truth: I love to run. I was reminded that it is something fun to do. I had put so much pressure on myself and felt too much stress to complete a race in a set time. As a result, I lost sight of the fact that running is fun. I had lost the excitement. Through adhering to my dad's advice and my coach's homework, I once again became excited about putting on my shoes and hitting my favorite trail.

My hope is that by answering this question you, too, will view your next run with excitement. Perhaps you too had a marathon experience not go as you wished. Whether the first eight miles of your race have gone according to plan, may your ninth mile be one of excitement. May it be a time in which you relax, take a deep breath, and get excited about what you are doing.

What about when we run through those dry patches in our relationship with God? It would be great to think that there have never been any difficult patches in my relationship with God, but that would be untrue. We are broken people living in an imperfect world. Decisions we have made have caused us to sin, and thus create separation between us and God. Though we don't often like to admit it, our sin is what often gets us in trouble and creates difficult situations. Tongues cannot be tamed, and harsh words are lashed out. Emotions cannot be kept in check, and we give in to impure desires. Full of pride, we believe we can do everything on our own. Anger is not properly taken care of and gives root to bitterness, resentment, and hatred. Regardless of the specific instance, sin has caused separation from God. That is, until Jesus came to Earth to do what no man was capable of doing. The only perfect, holy, spotless Son of God came to Earth to take the penalty for all mankind. In so doing, he paid the final debt that none of us could pay to bridge the gap between a sinful man and perfect God.

The price is paid. The battle has been won. The victory belongs to those who are washed by the blood of Jesus Christ. Relax. Stop.

Take a deep breath. Let those truths sink in. Don't simply allow them to sink into your head, but make sure they make their way down to your heart. I hope that gets you excited. I hope coming back to the cross and realizing that your sins are paid for gives you excitement.

While my words may provide a different insight and may present the truth in a new or alternative way, there is something exciting and life-changing about the Word of God. Therefore, I am leaving this chapter with various portions of Scripture that I hope will inspire, encourage, and excite you. May they remind you of the God we serve. Allow these portions of Scripture to ignite or re-ignite your passion to live out the calling you have received from our Lord.

For the dry and weary:

Jesus answered, "Everyone who drinks this water will be thirsty again, but whoever drinks the water I give him will never thirst. Indeed, the water I give him will become in him a spring of water welling up to eternal life."
—John 4:13-14

Then Jesus declared, "I am the bread of life. He who comes to me will never go hungry, and he who believes in me will never be thirsty."
—John 6:35

To those needing peace:

I (Jesus) have told you these things, so that in me you may have peace. In this world you will have trouble. But take heart! I have overcome the world.
—John 16:33

Do not be anxious about anything, but in everything, by prayer and petition, with thanksgiving, present your requests to God. And the peace of God, which transcends all understanding, will guard your hearts and your minds in Christ Jesus.
—Philippians: 4:6-7

EXCITEMENT

The power of the Lord:

But you will receive power when the Holy Spirit comes on you; and you will be my witnesses in Jerusalem, and in all Judea and Samaria and to the ends of the earth.
—Acts 1:8

I can do everything through him who gives me strength.
—Philippians 3:13

To the hurting:

Not only so, but we also rejoice in our sufferings, because we know that suffering produces perseverance; perseverance, character; and character, hope. And hope does not disappoint us, because God has poured out his love into our hearts by the Holy Spirit, whom he has given us. You see, at just the right time, when we were still powerless, Christ died for the ungodly. Very rarely will anyone die for a righteous man, though for a good man someone might possibly dare to die. But God demonstrates his own love for us in this; while we were still sinners, Christ died for us.
—Romans 5:3-8

Praise be to the God and Father of our Lord Jesus Christ, the Father of compassion and the God of all comfort, who comforts us in all our troubles, so that we can comfort those in any trouble with the comfort we ourselves have received from God. For just as the sufferings of Christ flow over into our lives, so also through Christ our comfort overflows.
—2 Corinthians 1:3-5

To those seeking a safe place:

I love you, O LORD, my strength, the LORD is my rock, my fortress and my deliverer; my God is my rock, in whom I take refuge. He is my shield and the horn of my salvation, my stronghold. I call to the LORD who is worthy of praise, and I am saved from my enemies. The cords of death entangled me;

the torrents of destruction overwhelmed me. The cords of the grave coiled around me; the snares of death confronted me. In my distress I called to the LORD; I cried to my God for help. From his temple he heard my voice, my cry came before him, into his ears.

—Psalm 18:1-6

God is our refuge and strength, an ever-present help in trouble. Therefore we will not fear, though the earth give way and the mountains fall into the heart of the sea, though its waters roar and foam and the mountains quake with their surging.

—Psalm 46:1-3

For the heart that is afraid:

So do not fear, for I am with you; do not be dismayed, for I am your God. I will strengthen you and help you; I will uphold you with my righteous right hand.

—Isaiah 41:10

Peace I leave with you; my peace I give you. I do not give to you as the world gives. Do not let your hearts be troubled and do not be afraid.

—John 14:27

To the lonely:

Be strong and courageous. Do not be afraid or terrified because of them, for the LORD your God goes with you; he will never leave you nor forsake you.... The LORD himself goes before you and will be with you; he will never leave you nor forsake you. Do not be afraid; do not be discouraged.

—Deuteronomy 31:6, 8

Therefore go and make disciples of all nations, baptizing them in the name of the Father and of the Son and of the Holy Spirit, and teaching them to obey everything I have commanded you. And surely I am with you always to the very end of the age.

—Matthew 28:19-20

EXCITEMENT

To the sinner:

This righteousness from God comes through faith in Jesus Christ to all who believe. There is no difference, for all have sinned and fall short of the glory of God and are justified freely by his grace through the redemption that came by Christ Jesus.
—Romans 3:22-24

For God so loved the world that he gave his one and only son, that whoever believes in him shall not perish but have eternal life. For God did not send his Son into the world to condemn the world, but to save the world through him.
—John 3:16-17

Holy Father, we thank you for your Word. It gives strength to the weary, peace to the disheartened, courage to the dismayed, hope to the sinner. Jesus, may the truth of your Word and the power of your Spirit fan a flame of excitement within our hearts. May our excitement be contagious to those who see us. Lord, I pray that your Word impacts our hearts and changes the very way in which we live. May we never be the same after encountering your Word and the truth it boasts. Thank you for continuing to walk with us, never giving up on us. Lord, it is an honor and joy to be your disciple. May our journey be one filled with excitement. Amen.

MILE 10
ADAPTABILITY

Sunshine is delicious.
Rain is refreshing.
Wind braces us up.
Snow is exhilarating.
There's really no such thing as bad weather.
Only different kinds of good weather.
—Author Unknown

"Though I am free and belong to no man, I make myself a slave to everyone, to win as many as possible. To the Jews I became like a Jew, to win the Jews. To those under the law I became like one under the law (though I myself am not under the law), so as to win those under the law. To those not having the law I became like one not having the law (though I am not free from God's law but am under Christ's law), so as to win those not having the law. To the weak I became weak, to win the weak. I have become all things to all men so that by all possible means I might save some. I do all this for the sake of the gospel, that I may share in its blessings."
—1 Corinthians 9:19-23

SUNSHINE. RAIN. HUMIDITY. Snow. Five miles. Twenty miles. Flat. Hilly. Sandy. Jogging. Sprinting. Strong. Weak. Runs come in all shapes, sizes and varieties. Energizing. Exhausting. Early morning. Late night. Alone. Groups. One must be willing and able to adjust to the different conditions and situations.

Democracy. Monarchy. Conservative. Liberal. Pro-Life. Pro-Choice. Pro-Immigration. Anti-Immigration. Democrat. Republican. From war to same-sex marriage to taxes, the list of differing viewpoints on politics continues to grow. Despite the differences in opinions regarding such issues, one must be willing and able to adjust to the different situations.

Coke. Pepsi. Coffee. Tea. Wine. Beer. Sports. Music. Poetry. Movies. History. Fiction. Non-fiction. Green Bay Packers. Chicago Bears. There is an endless amount of interests and hobbies that can occupy an individual's free time. Dogs. Cats. Reading. Writing. Knitting. Video-gaming. Photography. Building. Despite the differences in hobbies, we must be willing and able to adjust to different situations.

Throughout our times of running, adaptability is one of the most important qualities to have. Various situations will cross your path that you cannot control. The only thing you have control over is whether you will adapt and adjust to the obstacles in front of you. This holds true for your training as well as the day of your race.

One would like to think that every day of training will be ideal. The stars will magically align each and every moment you tie your shoes to go out and train. Sorry to bring bad news, but it does not happen that way. There will be days when your schedule is so busy that the only time you can squeeze in a run is before the sun rises. Not only do you awake to the annoying sound of your alarm clock hours before you want to crawl out of bed, you awake to the pitter patter of rain beating on your window. The night before you had planned to take a nice run on your favorite soft surface trail to help your aching knee. Yet with the rain coming down, you realize the trail will be too soft as it is now mud. You must modify your plans and run inside on a treadmill.

ADAPTABILITY

I faced this exact situation for what seemed like weeks while training for my third marathon. At the time I was living in Germany in a place that was at a high altitude; thus our weather patterns were extremely fickle. Seeing the sunshine made me think I had an open invitation for a dry run when it best suited my schedule. For a few days in a row at the same time I was lacing up my shoes, clouds were starting to hide the sun. As my foot hit the road, so did the rain. My co-workers laughed at the irony, while I quickly had to alter my plans. Bizarrely, this scenario happened more than once.

There were times when it was raining all morning, yet I needed to get my run in prior to lunch. I would head out and by the time the water had stopped pouring in my post-run shower, the rain had stopped outside as well. Again, this happened more than once and turned into an ongoing joke. After my runs, I would exclaim to my co-workers, "Don't worry. I am back from my run, so we all know it won't rain again today."

Throughout training, there will also be an occasional injury or complete lack of energy and enthusiasm. You must be able to adapt accordingly when unforeseen circumstances cross your path. Listening to your body is one of the most important things you will need to do while training for your marathon. If you feel sore and have pain, be willing to alter your training. Soreness is not an excuse for being lazy or skipping out on your regimen. But you must listen to your body and adapt accordingly to what it tells you.

When it comes to the day of your race, it is a day in which you must have a mindset of adaptability. As with any day of the year, you cannot control the weather on race day. I faced that issue when I ran my third marathon. It was the hottest April 3 ever recorded in Freiberg. As a result, I had to drastically alter my approach to the race. At Mile 10, the heat was taking its toll on me, and I had to abandon the plans and ambitions I had originally started with.

Weather isn't the only thing you might have to adapt to on race day. Fuel stations might be at slightly different places than you thought. Your first few miles might be faster or slower than planned. As mentioned in Mile 2, you might get boxed in early in the race. When these things happen, you must be patient and willing to rearrange your game plan.

Adaptability is not just an important training mindset. We must be willing to adapt to the people we meet through the journey of life. The individuals who make up our society have a wide range of beliefs and opinions, and occupy their time with a plethora of varied interests.

As brothers and sisters in Christ, it is our responsibility to minister to others. While that at times may seem impossible, two passages of Scripture written by Paul in his first letter to the church at Corinth prove uplifting and encouraging. One gives us a reminder that we belong to the Body of Christ, and the other highlights the importance of meeting these people where they are.

In 1 Corinthians 12, Paul addressed the topic of spiritual gifts and the functions of the Body of Christ. Through the first twelve verses, he highlighted different spiritual gifts, and in the remaining nineteen verses, he explained how those gifts were to be viewed within the bigger picture, the Body of Christ. Paul's encouragement to us is that everyone within the body has something to offer. Every person has a specific role. I love the way Paul phrased this in verse 17: "If the whole body were an eye, where would the sense of hearing be? If the whole body were an ear, where would the sense of smell be?" Paul followed this up with a profound truth we would all do well to remember when discouragement, doubt, or frustration seems to overtake our minds and hearts: "But in fact God has arranged the parts in the body, every one of them, just as he wanted them to be." Read that last part one more time: "… just as he wanted them to be."

Max Lucado has this to offer:

You were born pre-packed! God looked at your entire life, determined your assignment, and gave you the tools to do the job!

You do something very similar before you travel. You consider the demands of the journey and pack accordingly. Cold weather? Bring a jacket. Business meeting? Carry the laptop. Time with grandchildren? Better take some sneakers and pain medication!

ADAPTABILITY

God did the same with you. Joe will do research—install curiosity! Megan will lead a private school—an extra dose of management. I need Eric to comfort the sick—include a healthy share of compassion. Denalyn will marry Max!—instill a double portion of patience.

God packed you on purpose, for a purpose. [32]

When God created the individuals who would make up his body, he did not make mistakes. He carefully selected each individual, providing him or her with the tools and gifts he knew he or she would need every step of the way.

My mind often turns to sports to find analogies. I grew up in a sports-loving family. I often think of the movie *Miracle*, a phenomenal film that portrays the triumph of the United States Men's Olympic Hockey team in the 1980 Lake Placid Olympic Games. Early in the movie, we see newly-appointed coach Herb Brooks in Colorado with the nation's best amateur hockey players trying out for a spot on the team's roster. To everyone involved in the selection committee's surprise, Brooks selects his team within a few hours. His assistant seems baffled that he not only has the team picked, but that he has left off some of the more prominent names, to which Brooks responds, "I'm not looking for the best players, I'm looking for the right ones." A few scenes later Herb is confronted by an angry board member over the fact that the team has been selected in such a short period of time, without any consent from the higher-ups. To this Brooks replies, "Every one of those boys was chosen for a specific reason. I've studied film on each and every one of them. I've seen them. I've watched them, and I've coached many of them. And the ones I haven't, I've spoken with their coaches and a lot of scouts in the area."

In Psalm 139 we can see that God did the exact same thing with us. He did not have to study us or talk to our parents to find out what we are like, for he knew before were born. With that knowledge, he created us with distinct passions and abilities so that we could function within the Body of Christ. And, as Paul said, God orchestrated the Body just as he wanted it to be.

Within the ministry I am a part of in Germany, each year we face a good amount of transition and turnover among our staff. During my first three years here I had five different immediate supervisors. The transient staff proved to be difficult, yet I considered myself blessed in how God perfectly paired me and another co-worker, Chris. I am more knowledgeable about sports than Chris, so I tended to hang around some of the athletic guys more than he. Chris has a much greater passion and knowledge base about photography and computers than I do. He loved helping the guys out with their computers, swapping pictures, and giving tips on how to take better pictures. I drove him crazy, coming to him on a daily basis and saying, "Why is my computer doing this, can you help me?" If the students needed help tuning a guitar, they would run to Chris. If they needed a laugh, they would ask me to sing, because I am tone deaf. My strengths seemed to be his weaknesses and his strengths were my weaknesses. I was blessed by the way in which we functioned and complemented one another. However, I could not always sit back and operate within my realm of "expertise." It was not uncommon for either one of us to step out of our comfort zone, adapt, and meet the students where they were.

In the same way, through his writing to the church in Corinth, Paul encourages us to step out of our comfort zones and adapt to those around us. The church back then, just like today, was comprised of people of different cultures, varying interests, and distinct ideas. What was Paul's answer to the diversity? "I have become all things to all men so that by all possible means I might save some."[33] Paul was willing and able to appropriately adjust depending upon whom he was trying to reach. To the Jews he became like a Jew. To the weak he became weak. Paul went out of his way and adapted in order that he might better identify with those he was trying to save. He did not sit back and wait for them to come to him. Rather, he took the initiative and proper steps so that he might save some.

We began this chapter looking at the differing viewpoints individuals may hold. While you are planted firmly in your opinion, your neighbor, your classmate, or your co-worker may be on the

ADAPTABILITY

other side of the fence. How will you take Paul's words to heart, and adapt and modify in order to reach others?

While we may be more prone to associate with those who are similar to us, we must be willing and able to adapt to and interact with those we do not easily associate with. If we choose to ignore those around us, we deny them the opportunity of hearing about the Gospel of Jesus Christ. And if we are waiting for them to come to us, it is the same as waiting for the perfect run, where the temperature is just right, the time to run is available and perfectly matches your distance, your legs are feeling fresh, and your mind is sharp and ready for a run. Certainly those runs come to us every now and then, but the majority of the time we do not face those circumstances. Accordingly, we must adapt and modify. In the same way, every now and then, the stars align and we are faced with a perfect situation in which to share the Gospel. Yet when things seem less than ideal, we must modify, adapt, and push forward, for it is in those moments that we find that God is our strength.

Holy Jesus, we thank you for the way in which we are carefully and wonderfully made. You designed us for a specific reason and with specific gifts and talents. Each member of your body has been called to certain tasks and we are thankful that you have equipped us for all the tasks that will come our way. Father, create in us hearts and minds willing and able to adapt when circumstances do not seem ideal. Holy Spirit, guide and direct us; encourage us to seek those who are lost so that we may save some. Encourage us to meet them where they are, knowing that you will guide, protect, and strengthen us. To your name be all glory and honor. Amen.

MILE 11
STRENGTH

"Ability is what you are capable of doing.
Motivation determines what you do.
Attitude determines how well you do it."
—Lou Holtz

"It's not the size of the dog in the fight that matters.
It is the size of the fight in the dog."
—Mark Twain

"Go, gather together all the Jews who are in Susa, and fast for me. Do not eat or drink for three days, night or day. I and my maids will fast as you do. When this is done, I will go to the king, even though it is against the law. And if I perish, I perish."
—Esther 4:16

JACK TOOK ONE look in my eyes and knew he was in trouble. I had finished lacing up my shoes, done a few quick stretches, set my watch, and looked at him with a twinkle in my eye that said "Are you ready for this?" Whether he was ready did not really concern me much. He knew it without my saying it.

I had been making good progress in my marathon training, and Jack and I happened to cross paths on the day of the week in which I was supposed to do a ten-miler. The course we chose was hilly. It was high noon and the thermometer was closing in on triple digits.

Jack is a true friend, one of the closest companions I have. He has journeyed with me through thick and thin. An example of Jack's friendship was made evident by his willingness to run with me on this particular day. He is a great athlete and a good runner. At that point in time, though, our training was drastically different. I was training for a marathon; he was training for a 5k. I was training long and slow; he was training short and fast. Despite the many elements against him, he decided to entertain me and run alongside me.

Before we even started running, Jack could sense the determination in my demeanor. This was not simply a pleasure run, but a training run that had purpose and value. As we started, he looked at me and said, "I think I'm in big trouble. Not only do I have to run against the strength of Tommy's body, which is in far better shape for this than mine, but I have to run against the strength of Tommy's mind."

In running, physical strength is a necessary asset to help propel you to reach your goals. Running hills is a great way to build strength in your legs and core. The journey up the hill is difficult, but there are few feelings greater than the burning sensation in your legs as you reach the summit.

I learned the thrill of running hills at a young age. It all started at Hospital Hill in Wisconsin as my dad and I re-created "Reggie White workouts." Hospital Hill was later replaced by Stratham Hill in New Hampshire. At Stratham Hill we found a steep trail about 100 yards long that led up to a gradual hill of about another 200 yards. Our routine was such that I would jog to the bottom of the steep hill while my dad would remain at the edge of the gradual

STRENGTH

hill. He would then watch me run up the steep hill, and as I closed in on 15 or 20 yards from where he was, he would take off and start running up the 200-yard gradual hill. I would emerge from the trail and follow him up the gradual hill and attempt to overtake him before he reached our imaginary finish line. The combination of speed work and hills proved to be a great workout for both of us. The steep hill required much physical strength in my legs. Attempting to chase him down in the final 200 yards helped to tone a mental strength inside of me.

Another workout I enjoy and have found to be very beneficial in building strength, both physically and mentally, can be accomplished on a treadmill. I am not the biggest fan of treadmills, but find them to be optimal at times if the weather is poor or if I want to closely monitor my pace. The treadmill allows you to change an easy five miles into a difficult five miles, if you so choose. On a treadmill, the key is to start at a speed that is slightly faster than your comfort level. I maintain this speed for 1.5 miles, serving as a warm-up. Then I step off the treadmill to grab a quick stretch if necessary and to mentally prepare for the remainder of the run. At the 1.5 mile marker, I increase my speed by one level (*e.g.*, from 9.2 to 9.3) and at the same time I increase the level of incline a whole level (*e.g.*, from 0.0 to 1.0). I do this a couple more times so that by the time I reach mile 2.5, I have increased my pace from 9.2 to 9.6 and have increased the incline from 0.0 to 4.0. Mile 2.5 serves as my summit, and I maintain this level of difficulty for another quarter mile until I am at 2.75 miles. Once at 2.75, I start to slowly decline. I drop the speed at the same rate I increased it. However, I decrease the incline only half as fast as I increased it so that when I run five miles, it isn't until the 4.5 mile mark that I am back to running at my original pace and original incline, giving me a half-mile to cool down, though at that point the original speed seems much more difficult than it originally did.

Not only is physical strength necessary to train for and run a marathon, but so is mental and emotional strength. Mentally, you must be determined to do something different, something special. Not everybody can pick up and start training for a marathon. It takes strength *and* determination. You must be strong emotionally, knowing you will tire. You will wear down physically, but your inner strength will propel you and keep you going. Mark Twain nailed it with the quote at the start of the chapter. We will all be gifted with different abilities, different strengths, and different capabilities. Those can separate the "boys from the men," but ultimately what matters is what you hold inside. How far are you willing to push yourself? How strong is your mind? How determined is your will?

I have found that Mile 11 is the first, but certainly not the last, time in which it is necessary to call upon this inner strength. At Mile 10, we "adapted and adopted" based upon circumstances that were out of our control. It is now time to dig inside and allow your brain and will to overpower the messages of fatigue you may be hearing. Borrowing a quote from the great movie *Chariots of Fire*, "The will to win comes from within."

One way to help yourself overcome and engage your inner willpower is to recite a few running mantras throughout your training that will give you the boost you need. Running mantras are short phrases that are personal to you, are easy to memorize, and provide you with an intrinsic sense of motivation to push you forward. One mantra I have used often is, "I am a machine." In my mind, machines are mechanical, fluid, and consistent; they do not break down, tire, or easily deteriorate; and they keep going (provided that they are fueled). As I run and grow tired, I whisper this phrase to myself and shortly thereafter find myself almost in a trance, pushing through pain step by step.

Another mantra I enjoy stems from my love of studying history. Upon securing victory in modern day Turkey, Julius Caesar was quoted as saying, "Veni, vidi, vici," which translates to "I came, I saw, I conquered." It was my hope and intention that I would come to the race and conquer whatever it threw at me. It was my job to conquer the race, not let the race trample over me. Those are two mantras I have used. You should find mantras that are personal and fitting for you.

What are some basic guidelines for creating a mantra? Keep it short. You do not necessarily want to be reciting an entire

STRENGTH

Shakespearian monologue. Five or six words should be the maximum. You just need a phrase that will evoke emotion and allow you to channel some of that inner willpower. A small mantra is also easier to write on a wristband come race day.

Make it personal. Again, what works for me is not necessarily going to work for you. Studying history excites me. It is something I enjoy. Therefore, having a mantra stem from a significant historical character taps into other passions I have outside of running.

Remember the positive. You will want mantras to help you out when you are struggling, but you will also want a mantra or two to help pat you on the back or give you an inner high-five. "I am a machine" served me well when I was running well. When I felt light on my feet, when hills didn't seem big, and when everything was flowing, I felt like a machine, and I rewarded myself by telling myself how I felt.

Experiment. Some mantras will work, some will not. You will be doing plenty of training runs, so don't be afraid to test them out while training. You don't show up on race day and on a whim decide to run in a different pair of shoes. Similarly, don't show up on race day thinking you will come up with mantras on a whim as you run.

Have fun. Be creative. Draw inspiration from books, music, movies, Bible verses, posters, historical characters, etc. Allow the mantra to represent a part of your personality. Write it on a mirror where you will see it daily, or write it down in a running journal.

At times when I am reading the Scriptures, my imagination takes over. I like to try to envision the characters in the stories to make them come more alive. I wonder, did some of these people, and some of the individuals who penned the Holy Scriptures, have mantras? Joshua heard from the Lord as well as Moses, "Be strong and courageous."[34] How many times did he repeat those words to himself as he was marching around the walls of Jericho?

David was not foreign to his share of difficulties and painful situations. How many times did he whisper to himself, "The Lord is my shepherd"[35] as he went from cave to cave as a refugee, with a king hoping to take his life at any opportunity?

Nehemiah faced opposition on many fronts. When the mocking cries came or accusations against his reputation suppressed him, I imagine him whispering, "The gracious hand of my God is upon me."[36]

Isaiah, a prophet commonly faced with discouraging situations, would exclaim, "Do not fear, for I am with you. Do not be dismayed, for I am your God."[37]

While the Scriptures are flooded with great mantras, there is one that, for me, stands apart from them all. The words do not come from a mighty king. The author is not one who physically walked alongside Jesus. The author was not among the society's elite. In fact, this individual came from one of the lowest of the lows who was open to God's calling and was mightily used by Him. The author was a Jew in a foreign nation. Low. She was an orphan, taken in by an uncle. Lower. The author was a she, not a he. Lowest (culturally speaking, of course). Yet none of that mattered to God. What mattered was the inner strength and determination she held, which can best be summed up in what I consider her life mantra, "If I perish. I perish."[38]

Before we uncover Esther's mantra, it is important to recognize her situation. She was living under the reign of Xerxes who had an empire that encompassed 127 different provinces. Among these different provinces, there was a vast array of people, customs, and ways of life. Though there were seemingly many different groups of people, the evil villain, Haman, had a grudge against the Jews. We get to see a small portion of a conversation between Xerxes and Haman, which reveals part of the Jews' and Esther's strength:

> There is a certain people dispersed and scattered among the peoples in all the provinces of your kingdom whose customs are different from those of all other people and who do not obey the king's laws; it is not in the king's best interest to tolerate them. If it pleases the king, let a decree be issued to destroy them, and I will put ten thousand talents of silver into the royal treasury for the men who carry out this business.[39]

STRENGTH

It might not stand out as to why this passage speaks of strength; perhaps reading it again will help. It is fascinating that the Jews stood out to Haman because they were different. That one word, tucked away in a conversation of rage, sheds great light into the Jewish culture. To be different means "to be set apart, having none that is alike or equal." It took great strength and determination to be set apart in a society filled with pagans, idols, pleasures, wickedness, and filth. Yet Esther and her family did just that. Recognize that the words "different" and "holy" share commonalities in their definitions; the words "set apart" are used to define both.

Do you believe people notice something different about you? Is there something different about your conduct, your speech, or your way of life that makes people scratch their heads and say, "He is different." Now by different I don't mean, "Look at him … he's weird." I mean different in the fact that they can visibly and audibly recognize that Jesus Christ is an active presence in your life. As you read through Esther's story, you will find that she was in fact different from those around her. I pray that you, too, will have the inner strength to be different despite what your culture and society expects out of you.

Another way Esther displayed strength was in the way she was willing to ask for help. That does not sound normal. It sounds abnormal. It sounds … different. Many believe in the mantras "I am number one" or "I am superman" or "I don't need anybody's help, I can do it on my own." Some subscribe to the idea that "asking for help is for weaklings." We stand there, act tall and strong, and say, "BRING IT ON."

Esther was different. Faced with a task too big to carry alone, she pleaded to her uncle Mordecai, "Go, gather together all the Jews who are in Susa, and fast for me. Do not eat or drink for three days, night or day. I and my maids will fast as you do."[40] Recognizing the monumental task ahead of her and the implications behind it, she wanted to make sure her family and friends were aware of her situation and were there to help her. She was not too proud to disallow anyone to see her emotion; rather, she was open and honest about the task at hand. It takes strength to be open, honest, real, and vulnerable.

We were not meant to do it alone. We were not meant to tackle every obstacle that comes our way by ourselves. We are the body of Christ. We are in this together; we are on the same team. Do not be so strong and naive to think you can do it on your own. There will be tasks that will come your way that require you to ask for help, to ask for guidance. Do not be so proud, so ignorant, that you don't ask for help.

Following her words admitting she needed help, we come to what I have called her mantra, "If I perish, I perish."[41] Esther was about to enter the king's presence without being summoned by him, which easily could have translated into immediate death. She was stepping into a room unaware of whether she would come out alive. If she were fortunate enough to have her life spared, she had a plan to reveal to the king that she was a Jew, the very people about to be mass-murdered. Listen to those last words, "I will go, even though it is against the law, and if I perish, I perish." She knew full well what she was getting herself into. She knew what she had signed up for. Yet this did not deter her determination. She knew what could happen, but she had decided to move forward. What determination! What strength!

Strength and determination—two characteristics that perfectly define Esther. Two traits our society could use more of. While I have been encouraged to read through Esther's story and see the way in which she lived out these two traits, I have been more impressed and inspired by the way in which I have seen these characteristics lived out by my mom. Strength and determination permeate every breath she takes. Her inner strength and resolve are unmatched. Her determination and ability to love are unique and inspiring. Our family has been through a few storms, yet each and every time Mom was there to love, support, and encourage. She was by my dad's side for every one of his chemotherapy sessions. There to provide laughter when he needed it. By his side shedding a tear to empathize with him. Holding his hand to ensure he knew he was not alone. When my sister was in the hospital, if there was only one

STRENGTH

person by her side, you could be confident it was my mom. She was in the hospital room praying, talking, listening, encouraging. She was in the car driving, ensuring I did not miss a game. She was in the classroom teaching, educating, mentoring, and inspiring. She has faced many challenges where giving up might have seemed tempting—yet that thought never crossed her mind. Her hope in Jesus gave her strength and determination to keep going regardless of outside circumstances.

We may not find ourselves before a king who has the power to instantly kill us. We may not find ourselves in a hospital room watching a spouse fight cancer. However, whatever difficulty may be before you, whatever trial you may have, keep your eyes directly forward, focused on the goal with unwavering concentration until it has been accomplished.

Jesus, I thank you for your Word and the inspiration and strength it provides us. I thank you for the lives of the men and women you chose to highlight to help guide us along the path. Father, I believe that Esther was a woman of great strength. She asked for help when she needed it. She was also determined. She was focused. She was different. I pray that your Word and your Holy Spirit would fill us with the same strength and determination to tackle whatever obstacles currently stand in our way. Amen.

MILE 12
TRUST

"Trust yourself, then you will know how to live."
—Johann Wolfgang von Goethe

"Trust your training."
—Anonymous

"The woman said to him, 'Sir, give me this water so that I won't get thirsty and have to keep coming here to draw water.'"
—John 4:15

THIS WORLD THROWS plenty of situations our way that cause us to be uneasy, highly excitable, apprehensive, anxious, and nervous. Being on stage in front of a large number of people. Driving in traffic while a storm pummels the area with snow. Days that feel like years as you wait for the doctor to return your call about the test results. Being outside in the dark. Being alone. Asking a girl out on a date for the first time. Those last few moments before kick-off at the big game. The butterflies flutter around in your stomach. The nervousness your body feels through all of these situations and more is not unlike the nervousness you may encounter during Mile 12.

What if I didn't train long enough? What if I didn't train hard enough? What if I followed an untrustworthy training plan? Did I taper enough? Did I eat the right breakfast the day of the race? Am I going to be able to hold the food down with the whirlwind of emotions I am experiencing? How much did I drink before the start of the race? Was it enough? Was it too much? How is the weather going to affect my run? Is the sun going to drain my energy? Is the rain they predicted going to come, and if so, will it help or hurt me? What if I hit "the wall"? When will I hit the wall? Will I be able to recover? What if my running partner wants to push harder and faster than me? What if … ? What if … ? What if … ?

What if I've committed more sins than anyone could possibly forgive me for? What if someone knew all the thoughts that ran through my head? What if I never overcome this addiction? What if I lose my job? How will I pay the bills? How will I provide for my family? What if my spouse one day decides she is no longer in love with me? What if I ask, and she says no? What if I don't have the support of her family? What if nobody ever loves me? What if someone found out what I do when everyone else is asleep? What if … ? What if … ? What if … ?

Mile 12 is upon us. Almost halfway. Close to overcoming the mental hurdle of knowing you have more behind you than in front—but you are not quite there. For the 5,280 feet that separate you and that mental hurdle your mind will be throwing in your way, you must fight the seeds of doubt. At this point in the race you may start to get anxious; anxious about whether you trained enough or too much.

The twelfth mile can also be a very quiet mile, giving doubt added volume in which to intrude your thoughts. The silence is similar to that of the taper period. Tapering, which occurs in the last couple weeks of your training, is all about resting and allowing the body and mind ample time to recover and rejuvenate in time for the race. Tapering also enables the doubts to rev up. So it is with Mile 12. The thirteenth mile is typically a place of celebration for having reached the halfway point. Many runners might even be exiting the race if they are only running a half-marathon. But your race continues, and throughout this mile, so may the doubts, fears, nervousness, and anxiety.

At Mile 12, it may be that not everything has gone exactly according to plan. Something is probably a little off schedule. Perhaps you are off your target pace and wondering whether you will be able to make up the lost time. Some may find themselves feeling uncertain as to whether their breakfast was sufficient. Eating prior to a marathon is a bit of a science. Enough food needs to be consumed to ensure you do not quickly burn out; too much can create extra weight and perhaps other digestive problems.

When you begin Mile 12 you realize that you are one mile away from the halfway point. That halfway point will serve as a checkpoint. You will monitor your time and compare it to your target time. You will gauge your energy and stamina and assess whether you can repeat what you just did. With every step of Mile 12 you will be debating with yourself as to whether you trained the way you should have and whether you have the strength to continue. It is important to fight any nervousness and anxiety you may feel and kick the doubts to the curb. You must trust. Trust your training. Trust your plan. Trust yourself.

Since our childhoods we have been told to search for the fairytale life story. Movies provide images of romance with couples falling in love and living happily ever after. The radio plays music to dance away our problems. Society tells us we are to live our dreams and anything less is unsatisfying and unfulfilling. While many may wish for that type of life, it rarely happens. Circumstances do not always pan out in our favor. Hearts get broken. Illnesses happen. Children rebel. Jobs are lost. Bank accounts get depleted. Mortgages swallow housing equity. There are countless storms capable of crippling even the most grounded individuals. You must trust.

 I love the movie *Gladiator*. At one point in the movie, one of the characters poses the question, "Have you forgotten what it was like to trust in someone?" Trust is such a valuable thing. Trusting myself and others doesn't always comes easy for me, and I am likely not alone. One of the girls I coached at soccer in Germany exhibited an unbelievable sense of trust. This player redefined my definition of trust. She is an all-around athlete, with more experience playing basketball than soccer. However, during many soccer practices and games, she would come to me and ask, "Am I doing this right? What should I be doing different? How can I be more effective? Do you have any tips for me?" I do not claim to know everything about soccer. I am still learning about the game every day. Sometimes I do not know that I trust what I am telling players. But this player would listen to what I said, trust that I had her and the team's best interest at heart, and then attempt to go out and accomplish what I told her. It was encouraging and challenging to see someone exhibit such trust in another person.

 There is another woman who exhibited an immense amount of trust, which once again challenged me to ponder my own personal level of trust. After seeing her, it was obvious that her entire world was different because her heart trusted the words that were spoken to her.[42]

 Her name was never revealed even though her testimony has impacted untold millions. She carried a backpack full of nervousness and fear. She appeared in the middle of the day, in the beaming heat. Logic tells us that this was a bad time to venture off. The safe and sane thing to do was to remain inside, grab some shade and a glass of lemonade, and take an afternoon siesta. Yet this is precisely why she decided to gamble and head out. Assuming all others would be taking a siesta, she figured she could fill her water jug without hearing the sneers of her neighbors.

TRUST

She treaded softly through the streets, hoping not to wake or stir anyone. She moved from shadow to shadow, hoping to remain as invisible as possible. Upon crossing paths with another human, her head dropped in shame and embarrassment. Afraid of making eye contact, her shoulders dropped, forcing her eyes to firmly gaze at her feet. She had been the talk of the town for quite some time and had grown weary of walking through the streets and feeling every eye turn toward her as she witnessed people whisper, chuckle, and point at her. She wondered …

What if I hadn't made so many poor choices?

What if somebody could actually love me?

What if I could become good enough for someone else?

What if I can never get out of this miry pit I have created for myself?

What if I could just start over?

What if someone knew about all of my hurts and pains?

What if someone could see beyond the mask I put up?

What if someone knew all of the things I have done? If someone knew, how could they possibly love me?

What if … What if … ? What if … ?

She had no intention of ever telling anyone all she had done. The dirty laundry list was far too long. She couldn't imagine she would ever find anyone who would care enough to know everything. She could not comprehend someone having enough time and patience to listen to such a long list. She couldn't trust someone with that much information. The leverage they would hold over her made her mind spin and heart break. The weight of simply thinking about someone else knowing so much was almost too much to bear. She could never envision herself revealing all of her secrets to someone. Laughing to herself over the absurdity of the question, she neared the well. But as she approached the well, her nervousness took on a whole new meaning.

It was not another woman from the town waiting to mock her that sent chills down her spine; it was a man. The woman had seen a lot of different men in her life but this one she did not recognize. To make things worse, the stranger was a man of a different race. Not simply any other race, but the race she was indoctrinated to hate from before she could walk. They were to eat separately, wear clothes that distinguished them from each other, and live in separate sections of the city; everything about them was to be different, for they despised one another. The man approached her and asked her for a drink of water. She was confused, startled, intrigued, and nervous.

In response to his request, she asked him why he, a Jewish man, would make this request of her, a Samaritan woman. It is interesting that this woman answered his request with a question. It was as if she was uncomfortable with the ball being in her court and she wanted to pass it right back. She did not know how to best handle his request. What was proper etiquette in this situation? Little did she know that her nervousness was going to lead her out on a plank, forcing her into one of two options—to trust and have her life changed, or to distrust and carry on with the life she had been living.

Her question prompted the man to slowly reveal who he was and what he had come to accomplish. While he may have been physically thirsty, his initial request had very little to do with wanting a drink of water. His goal was not to force the woman to search the depths of the well. His goal was to prompt the woman to search the depths of her soul. He knew that deep down the well had rushing water. He also knew that the deep caverns of this woman's heart were parched. As water can quench a dehydrated throat, this man was offering that which could saturate the most arid of hearts.

For quite some time the woman had been going from house to house, man to man, searching for a way to fill a longing in her heart. Yet with each stop she made, the hole could not be filled. It only seemed to grow larger and deeper. She was looking for something that no ordinary human could produce. She was searching for something that was never fading. Something she had been searching

TRUST

for but had yet to take hold of. Something far greater than anything this world could offer; so great that it must be out of this world. Fortunately for her she was conversing with someone from out of this world, the Son of God.

    Jesus offered the woman the opportunity to partake in the water that would spring up, welling into eternal life. Can you imagine the excitement that must have been bursting from this woman? Everything she had been searching for was sitting within arm's reach. Yet as soon as the excitement came it left, as Jesus summoned her to get her husband. Knowing she did not have a husband, her excitement turned to shame.

    As all her secrets were brought to light, nervousness coupled with her shame. Not yet fully aware to whom she was speaking, she could only listen as her faults were spoken of without ease and without holding anything back. As Jesus mentioned these things, her face likely turned red, not from the midday sun but from shame and embarrassment. Her eyes quickly glanced around her, wondering if anyone else was within ear shot. However, this time something was different. She did not feel eyes of ridicule and judgment glaring at her. In fact, she noticed the eyes sharing these secrets were full of love and compassion. There was an emotion she had never seen before. His voice sounded so different from the mocking cries of her family and townspeople. It had been a natural reaction for her to feel condemnation when her past came up. But this voice was filling her with hope and reconciliation.

    Following Jesus' next statement, the woman spoke of her belief in the coming Messiah, to which Jesus responded, "I who speak to you am he." Oddly enough there was no more written dialogue between these two. After Jesus' final words to the woman, the disciples came back and then the woman left. She left full of trust, truth, and encouragement. Initially, the feet that carried her to the well were full of fear, slow moving, attempting not to be seen or heard. Yet as she came back from the well she was completely different. No longer nervous. No longer enslaved by shame. She charged into town proclaiming all that had happened. When we first met her she was tip-toeing through the town not wanting to wake anyone. Now she was drawing as much attention to herself as possible in order to spread the news she had just received. "What ifs" ran through her mind as she walked to the well. The one that now made her chuckle was, "What if someone knew all of the things I have done? If someone knew, how could he possibly love me?" For the first time in her life she had met someone who loved her despite all that she had done. She walked away from her encounter with Jesus changed. She trusted. She believed.

Isn't it time that we, too, trust Jesus like this Samaritan woman? Lots of things in our world can cause us to doubt. However, we need to trust that Jesus has our best interests at heart. His word has promised that all things will work together for good, for those who love him.[43]

Here is a thought I have when my mind prevents my heart from trusting. You may fill in the blank at the end of the sentence however it best applies to you, whether it's in finances, marriage, children, education, neighbors, etc.

> I find it foolish that I am willing to trust Jesus to rescue my soul from eternal damnation in hell, yet I am not able to trust that he will take care of _____.

When we trust, it is not only our lives that will be changed, but the lives around us as well. For the story does not simply end with the Samaritan woman changing; rather, she goes out and helps others change. Following her conversation she runs and explains to family, friends, neighbors, or anyone who will listen. After hearing her story, and seeing the change in her, they too are changed.

What should you do when the storms of life hit? Trust. You may think it sufficient to trust in yourself, your abilities, your charm, or your résumé. Those things may carry you for a little while. Yet they cannot carry you like the loving arms of a God who became man and took away the sins of the world. All he asks is that you trust him. He asks that you stop looking elsewhere for answers; instead, fix your gaze heavenward. Rather than living lives of busyness, seeking command of everything, we are to be on our knees giving it all up.

TRUST

Seeking, communicating, trusting. The Savior is asking for us to abandon everything and follow him with hearts that are full of trust.

Does nervousness and anxiety plague you as you lead up to your big race? Are you forgetting to trust in the weeks and months you spent preparing to run 26.2 miles? Don't let anxiousness rob you of the joy of running this race. Are you nervous that God won't forgive you, or that he won't carry you through a certain season of your life? Trust in the heavenly Father. Don't forget how big he is or how much he cares for you.

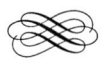

Jesus, thank you for being so trustworthy. Thank you for never changing. Father, you know our hearts are troubled and easily swayed. May the winds of nervousness not penetrate our hearts. May they never form a foundation in our minds. When we are tempted to be full of fear and anxiety, may your Holy Spirit overwhelm us with the peace that surpasses all understanding. Lord, I ask that we would continue to trust you with the seemingly big and seemingly small. You care for us and you love us. May we continue to trust in your unfailing love. Amen.

MILE 13
INSANITY

"Running is a mental sport, and we're all insane!"
—Unknown.

"What kind of crazy nut would spend two or three hours a day just running?"
—Steve Prefonatine

"Then the fire of the Lord fell and burned up the sacrifice, the wood, the stones and the soil, and also licked up the water in the trench."
—1 Kings 18:38

NUTTY. BIZARRE. LOONY. Batty. Off one's rocker. Intensely enthusiastic. Enamored. Infatuated. All can be used as synonyms for the word "crazy." Ironically, all can also be used to accurately describe the prophet Elijah. Wait a second ... am I talking about the prophet Elijah who is seen as a hero of the faith? The same Elijah who was fed by ravens? Yep, that's the one. He was crazy. Elijah, as in the prophet who defied all odds and went face-to-face with a queen (and then a king) who was readily killing any prophets she could find? Yes, that is the crazy man to whom I am referring. Elijah was a great prophet, and a crazy man.

In today's vernacular, the word "crazy" carries a few different connotations. On the one hand, "crazy" describes one who is slightly different—not really fitting into what we consider the "norm." For example: "Have you seen that teacher? She is crazy! She doesn't make any sense, and she makes the weirdest comments. I don't understand her; she is really bizarre." Crazy can depict something that is abnormal, something not commonly seen or experienced. When something is beyond our comprehension, it becomes crazy to us.

"Crazy" can also be used to describe the amount of energy, passion, or enthusiasm one has towards something. For example, "He is a crazy fan. He knows every player and watches every game. Don't watch a game with him, because when they score he will go crazy."

Crazy teachers. Crazy fans. Crazy runners. Join the club, my friend, for if you are running a marathon, you have a bit of craziness in you. The training regimen for a marathon is a monumental task to undertake. The time, energy, desire, commitment, and dedication that you must give to your training is beyond the "norm." There is no doubt you have spent at least two months training, running, and preparing for this one day, this one event. You have run in all kinds of weather and gone up countless hills. You are nutty.

After all of the training you have been through, you still had the enthusiasm and infatuation with running to approach the starting line. The difficult days, the sore legs, the weary muscles—none could not keep you away from the starting line. Now you are running through Mile 13.

INSANITY

I think you are at least slightly crazy and I mean that as a compliment. Trust me, being a crazy runner is a good thing. Running a marathon requires a bit of insanity. A few miles ago we encountered the emotion of excitement. As the first segment of the race was put to rest, you were renewed with energy and excitement. Now, a few miles after that happened, you can start to realize how crazy you are. For some, the craziness of the task at hand will not fully sink in until the race is over.

As we travel through Mile 13 together, we will embrace the craziness of the journey we are on. And I pray that through this chapter we can see our Lord and Savior as a little crazy, thus allowing us to fall more in love with him.

Elijah was a man who illustrates craziness. His life and his actions shed light into the attributes of a crazy follower of Jesus. His setting is not comfortable nor is it ideal for confrontation. Regardless of the circumstances, Elijah trusted and obeyed the Lord. He appeared before King Ahab, the very king who had been ruthless in his pursuit of any who did not worship the idol Baal. To Ahab and his kingdom, Baal was the god of rain, harvest, and lightning. Knowing the heart of the kingdom, Elijah walked into the king's presence unannounced, stating, "Over the next couple of years your kingdom will not see any rain nor dew unless I say so."[44] Elijah made this statement to a king who was actively killing people like Elijah, and openly challenged the one Ahab saw as God. Crazy. That one statement pinned a target on Elijah's back. If this scene had taken place in the Old West, there would have been hundreds of "Wanted Dead or Alive" posters placed around the kingdom with Elijah's face plastered on them. The underlying caption would have read, "Crazy man who believes his god can control weather."

We all seek adventure and thrill of some sort. Every now and then we need to accomplish something that fills our veins with adrenaline and excitement. Yet not many would satisfy this longing by going to a ruler and saying the exact words that would make us his number one target. Why did Elijah do this? He was being obedient to God. The amount of energy and enthusiasm he had to serve his heavenly King caused him to do something nutty, bizarre, crazy.

Following his interaction with King Ahab, Elijah continued to build his crazy-man résumé. The Lord said to Elijah, "Leave here, turn eastward and hide in the Kerith Ravine, east of the Jordan. You will drink from the brook, and I have ordered the ravens to feed you there."[45] What could have been going through Elijah's head and heart as he heard these words from the Lord? "I just challenged the king to his face, and now I am supposed to run away? Are you crazy?" Maybe he thought, "OK, I can go to the ravine. I can drink from the brook. But ravens? Are you messing with me? They are going to bring me food? And what do you mean by ordered?" God ordered the ravens. He commanded, he dictated, he instructed the ravens to carry out this mission for him. Crazy.

Think about some of the other individuals portrayed in the Bible. Moses was called to enter Pharaoh's court and inform him of the upcoming plagues. I wonder if he ever said to himself, "The entire Nile is going to turn into blood? That's crazy." Did David think as he ran towards Goliath, "I'm a little shepherd boy and there is a giant. Lord, I might be crazy but let's go for it!" Joseph heard that his fiancée, Mary, was pregnant even though they had yet to be married. To Joseph, that didn't seem possible. "Mary have a child? No, that's crazy!"

What about the thoughts running through your mind and heart right now? "Lord, you want me to talk to *him* about going to church? That's just crazy, he always makes fun of me for following you." Maybe you are being called somewhere like Elijah. "Jesus, I am supposed to sell everything I own, leave my family, and go *where*? I don't know that I could locate that country on a map, and I'm supposed to plant a church there?" Crazy. Yet like Moses, David, Joseph, Elijah, and many others, the crazy amount of energy and enthusiasm they had to serve their Lord led them to take the step forward. Their fervor for God inspired them to be obedient.

Elijah was crazy. His crazy obedience led him to a ravine where he was fed by ravens. After some time the brook ran dry and the Lord told him to go to Zarephath, home to many devoted Baal followers. There he met a widow who also appears a bit crazy. She and her son were dying of hunger, and then she met Elijah,

INSANITY

who asked for water and for her to make him some bread. With a heart that wanted to provide for her son, she was skeptical at first. But after hearing Elijah's promise that the oil and flour would not run out (sounds a bit crazy), she agreed. What Elijah asks of this woman was crazy, but she adhered to his request.

Following some time with the widow, Elijah was called to go back to Ahab, back to the land where he was a wanted man. He sought out Obadiah, a follower of the Lord who lived within the king's palace. Elijah requested that Obadiah enter the king's courts and inform the king that Elijah had been spotted within the kingdom. Upon hearing the request, Obadiah said to Elijah (paraphrasing), "Ahab has searched every inch of this country for you. He has not given up. He wants your head. He wants you dead. You want me to tell him I have seen you? That's crazy. How can I tell him without being killed? You want me to walk in and say, 'King Ahab, you know that man Elijah—the one you have been searching for non-stop? The one you put a bounty on and want dead? That guy you have been relentlessly searching for for the past three years? Well ... he's back. Yeah, he and I had coffee this morning. I have his cell number. Do you want it? He told me he wants to have a chat with you.'" Obadiah looked at Elijah and could only draw one conclusion. He was crazy!

As Elijah entered the king's presence, Ahab pointed a finger at him, blaming him for all the trouble within the kingdom. Like a madman signing his death warrant, Elijah fought right back and said, "Nope. Not my fault. Actually, it is your fault and the fault of your family."[46] This set the scene for a wild encounter between Elijah and his God versus the prophets of Baal and their god. Elijah was crazy with energy and enthusiasm knowing who his God was, and what his God was capable of.

Elijah picked a fight with Ahab, Baal, the prophets, and the nation. In so doing he gave every possible advantage to Baal. The venue? Mt. Carmel, Baal's home-court. The odds? Four hundred and fifty prophets to one Elijah. The task? Baal's specialty—a sacrifice requiring supernatural fire from the heavens. Baal was the god of weather and lightning. The sacrifice? Two bulls, of which

Baal's prophets had first choice. Every advantage was given to Baal and his prophets. What led Elijah to stack the cards in their favor? He was filled with energy, enthusiasm, and passion for his God. He was convinced that his God could accomplish what no other god was capable of.

Baal's prophets proceeded first and attempted to offer their sacrifice; yet nothing happened. After a few hours they began shouting, hoping that would help. Nothing. They started dancing. Nothing. At this point Elijah began taunting them. Sarcastic jeers poured from his mouth, meant to mock and frustrate Baal's prophets. Unsatisfied with the fact that their fire had not ignited, Baal's prophets shouted louder and began to cut themselves. After many hours there was still nothing. In fact, the people stopped paying attention.[47] It looked as though Baal was on vacation and was not going to show up.

Full of confidence, Elijah was ready to take the stage, draw back the curtain, and allow Yahweh to perform a miracle of which only he was capable.

Knowing that many had grown disinterested, Elijah summoned the townspeople to come near. He wanted them to see Yahweh's amazing display. He repaired the altar and invited Baal's prophets to fill jugs with water and pour it on the wood and the offering. Once again, Elijah was stacking the cards against him in order to further magnify God's power and majesty. After a prayer, "the fire of the Lord fell and burned up the sacrifice, the wood, the stones and the soil. And also licked up the water in the trench."[48] Game, set, match. Yahweh won. Baal and his prophets were defeated, humiliated, and disposed of. As the scene on top of Mt. Carmel comes to a close we are left with one final image of Elijah: "The power of the Lord came upon Elijah and, tucking his cloak into his belt, he ran ahead of Ahab all the way to Jezreel."[49] The distance is assumed to be around seventeen miles, a distance with which you will soon become familiar.

Elijah was a crazy man who was last seen in this story running seventeen miles. You are currently going through Mile 13 and it is an appropriate time to let you know this fact: you are crazy. It's a compliment, really. For someone to run a marathon is abnormal, something not commonly seen and something not commonly experienced. Additionally, to embark upon this adventure, you need a certain amount of energy and enthusiasm. It takes a bit of insanity to go through the rigors of training. If anyone looks at you funny or calls you insane as you talk about running 26.2 miles, take it as a compliment and look forward to being called crazy.

In this chapter we looked at Elijah and the way in which certain decisions he made must have seemed crazy at the time. In the same way, can you imagine what it was like for Jesus to leave heaven? I readily admit that I do not fully understand God's love, and I have often wondered and wanted to ask Jesus, "Are you crazy? You left heaven and all of its riches by your own choosing. You left the presence of the Father in order that you may come to earth for us humans? You traded all of heaven to save a people who will continually fall short, and cause pain, heartache and turmoil. You willingly chose to take all of our sin on your shoulders, a price you did not have to pay and a penalty you did not deserve. Why? Why did you do it?" Perhaps Jesus would respond with, "My love for them is abnormal, not common. It is full of energy, enthusiasm, and passion. It is never-ending, ever growing, undeserving, unconditional, life-changing, life-saving. Crazy."

P.S. Did I mention that at Mile 13 you're pretty much halfway there? Crazy.

Father, thank you for your love for us. It is indescribable. You left your place on high to come and die for sinful man. May our lives and the way in which we treat each other be nothing short of a reflection of your love. May you grant us strength, patience, and endurance when we need it so that all may come to know you. May our lives forever be changed because of your love. Amen.

MILE 14
FOCUS

"Never underestimate the power of dreams and the influence of the human spirit. We are all the same in this notion: The potential for greatness lives within each of us."
—Wilma Rudolph

"We all have dreams. But in order to make dreams come into reality, it takes an awful lot of determination, dedication, self-discipline, and effort."
—Jesse Owens

"His brothers then came and threw themselves down before him. 'We are your slaves,' they said. But Joseph said to them, 'Don't be afraid. Am I in the place of God?'"
—Genesis 50:20

THERE ARE VERY few, if any, regular commercials on TV that celebrate running. Television shows the basketball player soaring through the air, dunking, and leaving the backboard shaking. You can't miss the football player's bulging biceps and dazzling spins. Golf, tennis, NASCAR, and even soccer commercials flood the airwaves. And if the commercial isn't advertising the actual sport, its athletes are used as marketing tools. Usain Bolt, currently the world's fastest man, has only been in a few commercials in the U.S., but can you name one company that endorses Bolt? What about Lebron James? Peyton Manning? Roger Federer? As for those three, most likely you can.

We are in the age of the slam dunks, home runs, slap shots, 140 mile-per-hour serves, and 300-yard drives. Few are dazzled by a runner jogging down the road. Running, especially long-distance running, does not capture the attention of many. To most, it is unglamorous and boring.

What is it that attracts people to mainstream sports? Flashy uniforms? Cheerleaders? The dazzling grace of certain athletes? Their speed, power, and/or strength? What could be highlighted about marathon running? What would a running commercial boast about? The uniforms aren't dazzling. Marathoners do not flaunt flashy and bulging muscles. So what can be featured about marathon runners? Focus.

When the word "focus" is used, it refers to someone or something that has become the center of activity or attention. Focus describes that which is the central part of your attention. It is the point at which all elements and aspects converge.

Mentally envision a distance runner. The dedication and attention to detail is immaculate. Look in the eyes of the runner and you will see determination and focus. The marathoner needs focus every step of the way, for 26.2 taxing miles. Throughout Mile 14 you will be challenged to regain and maintain your focus. You must concentrate and adhere to that which has become the central point of your attention.

Running a marathon will push you. It will be a fight, most obviously in a physical realm. Many do not regularly run 26.2 miles,

FOCUS

so pushing the body for that distance is challenging. A marathon not only challenges you physically but mentally and emotionally. A marathon requires ALL of you. Every facet of your being. Through the fourteenth mile, the difficulty starts to kick in and become more obvious. You will likely have run greater distances than fourteen miles in your training, so hopefully the physical toll has yet to creep up on you. This is the point in the race, however, in which mental fatigue may attack.

Having just breached the halfway point, it is time to regroup and refocus. A focused individual has a central point of attention. Concentration and meticulous attention to detail help define what it is to focus on something. Through Mile 14 you need to focus on maintaining your discipline as a runner, and focus on limiting and hindering any and all distractions.

As discussed during Mile 2, one of the greatest attributes a marathon runner has is discipline. Yet as the miles add up it is easy to become undisciplined. It is easy to allow yourself to slip. Little by little you can lose your discipline.

Lack of discipline can be played out in a few different ways. By losing your focus, you may slowly start to drift from your desired pace. Remember in Mile 5 when we talked about having a goal? Right now you must focus and keep your discipline and not fall off pace.

It is easy to lose your discipline in the fundamentals of running. By now you should have a good understanding of the length of your stride and the rhythm of your breathing. If you become undisciplined, those things may fall out of sync and become unbalanced. Again, you may not see the impact of this immediately, however over time it will prove detrimental to your race.

Additionally, your running posture may start to suffer. Perhaps you were surprised at how sore you were following a long training run. Of course the legs were heavy the following day, but you never expected your upper back, shoulders, and biceps to be fatigued as well. As the distance increases it is common to allow yourself to slowly hunch over. Your shoulders can slowly move forward, closer and closer to the ground. You must maintain focus and not allow this to happen. Allowing your shoulders to hunch over will place an extra strain on the rest of your body and will prohibit your lungs from maximizing oxygen consumption. In a marathon, there are no timeouts. There is no halftime. You must focus the entire time.

If you lose your focus you may also lose your attention to other minor details. Prior to the race, minute details were attended to. Shoelaces were tied. Shirts and bibs were adjusted to exactly the right height. Notes of when to drink and what to eat were carefully made. However, at this point some of those details may have been put on the back burner. Do not allow yourself to lose focus.

When running my first marathon, I began the race extremely focused. My main concern was what the clock would say when I crossed the finish line. I was young, inexperienced, and unaware of the challenges ahead of me. But I was focused and determined. So focused, in fact, that I failed to pay much attention to things going on around me. There were close to ten-thousand runners enjoying the 26.2 mile journey, so much of the opening miles were spent surrounded by plenty of runners. Throughout the race I heard people on the side cheering and clapping. It was no doubt exciting and encouraging. It was great to be spurred on. Even better, occasionally I heard my name being called out! The first time or two it didn't really register as I was deep in concentration. But as the race progressed my ears were more attuned to my surroundings. After a few miles I started to pick up when people were clapping, cheering, and saying, "Go Tommy!"

The first time I heard my name being cheered, I looked around and noticed I was in a crowd of seven to ten other runners. I thought, "What are the odds that another runner in this group has my name? Probably pretty slim." A few miles passed and the running group dwindled. Even then, at the next water station I heard my name called out again. Confused, I looked around and didn't recognize anyone handing out water, and since our group had grown smaller the odds were even less that I was running with a fellow Tommy.

FOCUS

Somewhere around Mile 14 I found myself running alone, but thankfully there were still plenty of fans. Once again I heard people clapping and encouraging me … by name. Knowing full well I had no clue who they were, and there was clearly no other runner near me, I was puzzled. At the next water station I happened to glance down at my bib and right above my race number was my name. I laughed at how many miles I had completed before finally realizing this. Despite my embarrassment, I applauded myself for being so focused and not realizing something so obvious (or perhaps I was just naïve).

You just completed the thirteenth mile. As is the case with most marathons, you may have been given the option of veering off and finishing your race at 13.1 miles. However, continuing on means you head down the road that leads toward a full marathon. Your focus, your central point of attraction and concentration, must be on the road ahead.

Step away from thinking about your marathon for a moment. Where is the road headed that you are traveling down? What in life has become your focus? What holds your attention and concentration? What has crowded the street you are on and distracted you?

One of the most celebrated men of the Old Testament is Joseph, a man of focus. I believe he is held in such high esteem because his central point of attention was ensuring he glorified God, no matter the circumstance he found himself in. Joseph went through tough times in the prison, and Joseph went through beautiful moments in the palace. Yet regardless of his surroundings, Joseph focused on glorifying God.

Loved by his father, yet despised by his brothers. "Despised" might not be a strong enough word. Detested. Loathed. Rejected. Shunned. Hated. Abhorred. Combine those and you will get a glimpse of what Joseph's brothers felt every time they saw Joseph or heard his name spoken. Out of jealousy his brothers threw him in a pit. They left him to die, only to come back and think that selling him into slavery would bring them more reward (financial) and a less weighty conscience. Thus, Joseph soon found himself sold as a slave, and eventually in jail.

Would anyone blame Joseph if he were to give up, throw in the towel, and shake his fist at God? We almost expect Joseph to say, "It's about time I start doing things my way. I've tried to follow you and be in tune with you, and look where it led me—the bottom of a slimy jail. I could do a lot better if I did it my way."

Yet what did Joseph do? He kept his focus on God. He did not care about his surroundings, for whatever situation in which he found himself, he was going to focus on praising, serving, and loving God. As we follow Joseph's story, we find Joseph being put in charge of the prison. The warden trusted him. The Lord was with him, and he was with the Lord.[50]

For 730 mornings, Joseph awoke to the reality of living in a prison. These days were not comfortable for Joseph; yet they were beautiful. They were not easy; yet he remained focused. He paid close attention to how he could be a blessing to others, and how he could best glorify God.

One of my favorite scenes that we get to witness in Joseph's chapter of imprisonment comes from his interaction with the cupbearer and the baker. After some time they had the unfortunate privilege of joining Joseph in prison, and because of this their lives would be changed. The morning after these two individuals had dreams, Scripture tells us, "Joseph came to them the next morning, he saw that they were dejected."[51] He was not told they were sad, he could *see* their sadness. Joseph knew enough about these men, and he cared enough about them and for them, that he took the time to get to know them in such a way that he could simply *see* when they were upset. Words were not necessary. Isn't it amazing that even while Joseph was in prison himself, he had the focus and heart to care for others? He did not care for them because of what they could do for him. In fact, soon the cupbearer would forget about him for two years. He cared for them because of who they were in God's eyes.

Joseph showed his focus while in prison *before* we see him as a man of focus in the palace. There are those who find it easy to praise and worship God while things are going well. Yet the moment

FOCUS

things start to get a little bumpy, the praise dwindles. It takes a true man or woman of faith to praise God even while things are not going as well as we would prefer.

Two years after Joseph interprets the dreams of the baker and the cupbearer, he finds himself in front of Pharaoh interpreting his dream. As a result of Joseph's interpretation, Pharaoh says, "Can we find anyone like this man, one in whom is the spirit of God?"[52] Josephs' focus, heart, and dedication caused those around him to come to the conclusion that Joseph was connected with God. With his next breath, Pharaoh then declares that Joseph is in charge of all of Egypt. Everyone in the country is to submit to his orders.[53] Joseph was focused and caring while in prison. Now he finds himself with every material thing he could ever want. Yet the riches and pleasures of life do not cause Joseph to retract his focus from God and steer him to place his attention, his energy, or his thoughts on the material things. Joseph keeps God as the central point of his life.

With one final look at Joseph, we can once again see his focus. Toward the end of Joseph's life he is in the presence of his brothers, shortly after receiving the news that their father has passed away. His brothers are afraid that because their father is now dead, Joseph will seek revenge. However, rather than get even with his brothers, he encourages them by saying, "Don't be afraid. Am I in the place of God? You intended to harm me, but God intended it for good to accomplish what is now being done, the saving of many lives."[54] Joseph's main point of attention was to be a man who served and worshiped God, wherever he was, whatever he was doing. To him, there was no difference between the prison and the palace. They were both sanctuaries in which he was given an opportunity to love those around him and reflect the beautiful love of God. God desires for us to be where we might glorify him most. For some it will be a palace. For others, it will be a prison. Wherever you find yourself, focus on Jesus.

Lord, may you be the focus of all we do. May you be the center of our attention. Whether we find ourselves in a palace or a prison, may our lives reflect the truth that you are our focus. Amen.

MILE 15
PAIN

"I can endure more pain than anyone you've ever met.
That's why I can beat anyone I've ever met."
—Steve Prefontaine

"Marathoning is like cutting yourself unexpectedly. You dip into the pain so gradually that the damage is done before you are aware of it. Unfortunately, when the awareness comes, it is excruciating."
—John Farrington

"But he said to me, 'My grace is sufficient for you, for my power is made perfect in weakness.' Therefore I will boast all the more gladly about my weaknesses, so that Christ's power may rest on me. That is why, for Christ's sake, I delight in weaknesses, in insults, in hardships, in persecutions, in difficulties. For when I am weak, then I am strong."
—2 Corinthians 12:9-10

"Dear friends, do not be surprised at the painful trial you are suffering, as though something strange were happening to you. But rejoice that you participate in the sufferings of Christ, so that you may be overjoyed when his glory is revealed ... So then, those who suffer according to God's will should commit themselves to their faithful Creator and continue to do good."
—1 Peter 4:12-13, 19

PAIN

PAIN ... NOT MANY enjoy it. In fact, most of us run away from it when possible. Unfortunately, few, if any, are able to escape its grasp. You may be experiencing pain at Mile 15 ... or maybe not.

Pain can be defined as physical and/or emotional suffering or distress typically due to injury, illness, and/or a distressing situation. Physical pain rears its ugly face in a variety of circumstances and forms—headaches, pulled muscles, broken bones, toothaches, blisters, sores, dislocated hips, etc. Emotional pain can affect everyone in different ways and at different times: the loss of a loved one, the end of a relationship, lies from a gossiping tongue, etc. Regardless of the specific type of pain, one thing is almost certain—experiencing it is not pleasant.

I am not a doctor, nor do I claim to have any knowledge in the field of medicine. In fact, my motto throughout high school and college was "there is no injury that cannot be treated by taking ibuprofen and applying ice." Within the pages of this chapter, I will not go in-depth about running injuries, as I have little experience with respect to said topic. I have been fortunate and have experienced only a few running-related injuries, but there are a few things I would like to share. Hopefully you will find yourself encouraged and strengthened to tackle the situations around you.

Pain is not necessarily a bad thing when it comes to running. Inevitably we try to avoid it, but pain can be beneficial. Pain can warn you if you're injured or about to become injured. Also, "conditioning pain" can tell you if you're pushing yourself. In that regard, the cliché "no pain no gain" carries a lot of truth. In order to get stronger and to reach new levels you need to push yourself and in doing so will experience some pain.

Very few people enjoy running wind sprints "just because." I wish you could visit one of my soccer practices and listen to the groans when I inform the team "We are going to do our 7-5-3-1 sprints," or "Get in teams of three and leave the balls on the side." These few words instantly inform the team that we are running, and running hard. They will finish tired, out of breath, and with aching legs. They do not enjoy the pain. As their coach, it is not fun for me to see them breathless, hunched over, and grimacing in pain. I care for them, and want them to enjoy practice and playing. Yet as much as it hurts for me to see them go through pain, I believe it is in their best individual interests and the best interests of the team, because I know that when the next game comes they will be in better shape and better able to perform in the battle on the pitch.

Does God view us in a similar fashion? My love for my team cannot compare to God's love for us. My love is incomplete, impatient, at times conditional, and quick to keep record of wrongs. God's love is unconditional, pure, patient, trustworthy, hopeful, and persevering. God loved us while we were still sinners,[55] and he loved us before we loved him.[56] Though we constantly mess up, God's love does not run out. He is patient. While we may give up on him, he does not give up on us.

Though my love is imperfect, I hope that my love for those around me shines a light that points back to Christ. I hope that after I have had the opportunity to interact with those around me, they recognize there is something different and unique about me; something that points them to Christ and allows them to experience his good, perfect, and unconditional love. His love is so amazing that it understands and allows for pain.

A little over a year ago the pastor of the church I attend was preaching through the book of Luke. One Sunday he emphasized the phrase "There is no growth above the tree line." This hit my heart hard. Unintentionally over the next seven weeks I uttered that phrase to myself at least once every day. These words have given me a framework for pain and the way in which it shapes and defines us.

If you were to climb a hill or mountain, you would notice as your elevation rises that the amount of wildlife starts to dwindle. At the bottom of the trail you may look up at the trees and be amazed at their height. As you embark on the journey up, you slowly start to notice that the tops of the trees are not as far off as they once were. As you continue to travel up and the trees continue to shrink, you reach a point where you are level with the trees, perhaps even higher. At that point you have eclipsed the tree line.

PAIN

There is no growth above the tree line. There is no growth at the mountaintop. Hearing that created a bit of a paradigm shift for me. Prior to that, my thoughts were focused on climbing to a spiritual mountaintop. Getting to the place where your face is radiant and everything seems to be going right, quiet times are in abundance, prayers are deep and passionate, and new believers are joining the family. While those are definitely good, the phrase seemed to hold true—the greatest times of growth were not while I was on the mountaintop, they occurred when I was below the tree line. Not always standing and rejoicing on the mountaintop, but on my knees begging and pleading. Not always times of happiness and stress-free picnics, but times of pain, heartache, and confusion. Times when it seemed as though I was constantly running sprints, hunched over, tired, aching, and wondering when a time of refreshment was going to come. Times when I questioned where God is. Pain can be beneficial. Pain enables us to grow.

Have you ever come out of a life storm only to later look back and say, "There is no fiber in my body that desires to go through that again. Yet knowing what I know now, seeing how I have changed, recognizing how I have been shaped more into the image of Jesus Christ … I would gladly go back through it in order to come out in this way"? Pain can be beneficial. I am certain there were many times I learned this while growing up, yet nothing left a greater impression on me than the months leading up to and during my first year of high school.

For months my dad had been suffering occasional cramp-like pain in his abdomen. At first he thought it was some sort of latent bug that he may have picked up on an international business trip. He described it as a once- or twice-a-week episode of "morning sickness" that would go away (usually by vomiting) in time for his habitual daily noon run. Apparently I take after my dad, as he did not take it seriously and did not see a doctor to get the situation checked out.

One night he finally succumbed. The pain had come in the morning, as usual, but didn't go away that day. In fact, rather than going for his run at noon, Dad decided to take the afternoon off and "deal with the situation." The pain continued through the day and into the evening. That evening, a terrible storm blew through our neighborhood. Heavy rain and pounding wind blitzed the area. Dad's pain intensified, and much to the family's surprise, he suggested that perhaps he should go to the hospital. Outside, the power of the storm continued to increase. Thunder and lightning added to the intensity, causing power outages.

When Mom and Dad pulled the car out of the garage, they saw that the wind had ripped an enormous tree from our yard and threw it across our driveway, preventing any vehicle from coming in and out. In a humorous way my dad saw the tree and exclaimed, "This is God's way of telling me I'm just constipated and that there is no need to go to the hospital tonight."

However, the pain continued to get worse. The discomfort my dad was in became even more intense. We borrowed a car from a neighbor and my mom took my dad to the hospital. After arriving at the hospital, Dad went through a series of tests to pinpoint the reason behind the pain. I went to bed that night thinking everything was fairly normal. I was fourteen years old. I recognized there was a storm raging outside our house, but I could not see nor fully comprehend that one of the most difficult storms of our lives was just beginning.

I woke up the next morning to my mom kneeling by my bed, gently nudging me awake. She wanted to let me know my dad was still at the hospital and was about to go into surgery but that I should go to school as normal. Still half-asleep, I don't know that I fully heard or understood what she said. In one sense the next couple of hours and days were a blur, yet I feel as though I can vividly remember everything. My dad came out of surgery well, but they had found and removed a tumor. He was diagnosed with stage 3 colon cancer. This was something ibuprofen and ice could not cure; rather, chemotherapy was the plan of attack.

A few months after surgery the chemotherapy began. I tagged along for the first session, a day that will never be removed from my memory. There seemed to be an uneasy feeling among everyone. In an attempt not to show emotion and keep the mood as light as possible, jokes were told left and right, which is typical in our family. The session went well. In fact, afterward my dad and I went golfing. Full of ignorance, I felt as though this was what every Wednesday was going to be like. I couldn't figure out why everyone was making such a big deal over chemotherapy. Soon enough our family would figure out exactly how ugly chemotherapy can be.

I tried to remain ignorant for a while. I'm not entirely sure why. Most likely I thought that if I ran away from the problem and rejected the truth I would become immune to reality. As thought-out as my game plan appeared, it did not work. After a few weeks of chemotherapy, my dad gradually became weaker and sicker.

That summer I had the opportunity to travel to England and play soccer. We were there for ten days, one of which happened to be a Wednesday. It was the first time I was unable to go with my dad to a chemotherapy session, and despite the distance I wanted him to know I was still thinking about him. I managed to call home that day (which at the time was not nearly as easy nor cheap as it is today) and distinctly remember being in the hallway on the phone, saying to my mom, "I know today is Wednesday. Can you tell Dad I wish I were there with him today and not here?" To which my mom responded, "Tommy, I am glad you are there and not here. I don't want you to have to see your dad in the shape he is in." My heart sank. My world was crushed. Reality hit and hit hard.

I returned from England more in check with the reality of the situation. Reality brought with it fear, anxiety, worry, and pain. While it appeared as though the chemotherapy had a chance to work, my dad was getting increasingly sicker every week. I found myself waking up in the morning unaware if my dad was going to wake up and make it through the day. That was the reality in which I lived. That was the fear and pain that gripped my heart. Despite all my dad was going through, he continued to love, support, and encourage our family. There was one night in particular that left me speechless and in awe of a father's love, and speechless in fear of what chemotherapy was doing to my dad.

My dad's health made our entire lives far from normal for quite some time, yet as a family we found it helpful to be as normal as possible. Therefore when the fall sports season rolled around, my brother and I played soccer. Our sister was still young, but was involved in volleyball. As fall ended and winter came I played on the basketball team. One night we had an away game that normally would take about forty-five to sixty minutes to travel to. However, on this particular day there was a horrible winter storm dumping a lot of snow all over the roads. New Englanders are accustomed to driving in such conditions, but the length of the trip doubled as a result.

That particular day was a Wednesday, a day I knew my dad would be going in for chemotherapy. At this point in his treatment my parents no longer wanted me to go to the treatments, as my dad was getting quite sick—to the point that the hospital had given him a private room for his sessions. After my dad's treatment, he and my mom drove the long journey, fighting the weather to make it to the game.

I did not know this was going to happen, and did not expect it. In fact, I did not even look into the stands during warm-ups, thinking there was no chance they would show. Early in the first quarter of the game there was a free throw and I found myself lining up under the basket. I randomly happened to be in a box facing toward the stands. For a few moments I lost all focus on the game as I looked into the stands and saw my parents in the bleachers. My dad was sitting next to my mom. Tired and weak, he rested his head on her shoulder. When our eyes met, he raised his hand and gave me a big thumbs up. I was speechless. I was frozen. I don't remember if the shot went in or not; I don't remember if we won the game or not. I really didn't care.

After the game I immediately went to my parents and thanked them for coming. Then, without really thinking it through, in a rash tone I asked, "Why did you come to the game? Today is Wednesday. The weather is terrible. Why aren't you at home?" While elated they were there, I was concerned and worried. Following my question came an answer I will never forget: "Tom-Tom, if this cancer gets the best of me, I wanted to make sure I saw my son play one more game." I will never forget the love, the sacrifice, and the commitment shown by my dad that night. I walked out of the gym a champion—not because of anything I had accomplished on the court; after all, I cannot even remember who won. I walked out a champion because despite all the pain, fear, and worry I was struggling through, I knew I was loved by my father.

That is a realization that has changed my life forever. Not just life here on earth, but life in eternity. It was through those dark and painful days that my faith became my own. It was through the difficulty and uncertainty of that storm that I truly found Jesus as my friend, my companion, my Lord, and my Savior. For fourteen years I had acted in a certain way because it was the way I was raised. I had gone to church for fourteen years because that is what my family did. There was never any real passion or desire. It was more out of a routine that I went. Up until that stormy night I had been flying under the wings of my parent's faith. They raised me well, loved me, and nourished me. However, I had yet to come out from their wings and learn to fly on my own. When my dad was diagnosed with cancer I was hit with the reality that I could wake up and he would no longer be there. (In fact, that can happen to any of us at any point, but the presence of cancer seemed to make it more real.) As a result of coming to that realization I had to ask myself, "Is my faith something I really believe in? Am I going to allow this to completely change my life and define who I am, or is it going to simply be a part of who I am?" I do not know the specific day, hour, or where I was, but I know as a result of seeing my dad go through his sickness my faith in Jesus Christ became real. It became the driving force of my life, and the thing that defines me today.

With that knowledge I look back at those months with joy. They were not fun. Let me assure you they were full of fear, pain, worry, doubt, and frustration. Yet when I look at the way God worked through my life during that time, I would not trade those days for anything. I look back and am thankful for the pain. The pain was beneficial. Those dark days changed my life for the better. Not only here and now, but for all eternity.

God works in mysterious ways; ways that I cannot begin to understand. Sometimes I am grateful for that; other times I am confused, frustrated, and even angry. While there can be a lot of pain as you are sitting next to someone you love who is going through a difficult time, a lot of pain can occur from being away from a loved one in a painful situation.

The timing of writing this chapter is mysterious. A few days ago I started to map out this chapter, and last night began writing. Yet while at work today, I received a text message from my mom informing me that my sister and dad had taken our family dog, Duncan, to the emergency veterinary clinic. They were unsure of what was going to happen or his prognosis. (Some of you may chuckle at the love a family has for its pet, but Duncan had been with us for more than seventeen years. My dad often talked about how Duncan sensed his cancer and was able to comfort him. And when my sister moved into her own apartment, Duncan went with her and became her roommate. So the news of Duncan at the vet was a big deal.) As it was just a text message, there was not much information given. I was simply told that something was happening, and I should be praying. My mind instantly thought the worst. Be praying. Emergency veterinary visit. Above all, this was coming to me via text … by my mom! Parents are not always up-to-date on the most recent technology, so when they use it, you know they are trying to communicate something vitally important. Much to my dismay, everything in my world here in Germany kept moving forward at a hundred miles per hour, when all I wanted was to derail and be with my sister. Students continued to come in my office; emails had to be sent out. For the next few hours I kept an eye on my texting device, hoping my mom would give me an update and more information. A few hours after the initial text, I received an email from my dad and the subject simply read, "Duncan's last day."

At first I didn't read anything he wrote. I just stared at the screen. I didn't want to believe it. Eventually I opened the email. As soon as I opened it my eyes swelled up with tears. I found myself staring out the window, hoping to distract myself. Looking back at the screen, I saw my dad had attached a picture; a picture of my sister, Whitney, and Duncan. Though you could not see all of Whitney's face, you could see enough to tell she had been crying. You could tell her heart was crushed and full of pain. And here I

PAIN

was thousands of miles away in Germany, knowing my sister was going through a very emotional and difficult day.

I felt helpless. Angry. Frustrated. Confused. There was great sadness knowing that Duncan was no longer a part of our family. He has been our dog for the past seventeen years. We picked him up from a breeder when my older brother Philip was nine, I was seven, and Whitney was five. Duncan was with us in Wisconsin as we were growing up. He moved with us to New Hampshire and became a source of comfort for us kids as we were in unfamiliar territory, with a new school, new friends, and new neighbors. He was there to listen to me cry as I worried over my dad's health. He was physically small, yet a big part of our family. Over the past few years he had been living with Whitney, keeping her company. Most recently, he had become an older brother to Whitney's new puppy, Ziva. He was a huge part of our family. A great dog. Fun. Energetic. Comforting. Loyal.

Though I was saddened by Duncan's passing, I was especially having a hard time being away from my sister at that time. I wanted to be there for her. I wanted to be there with her. I was able to call and talk to her for a few minutes. We laughed as we told old stories. We cried. It is difficult to be next to someone while she is visibly and audibly dealing with emotional pain. It is exponentially more difficult when there are miles separating you and months between the next time that you will be face to face.

Shortly after hearing about Duncan, I sent an email to two of my closest friends. These two guys have walked through life with me for quite some time. They have always been there when I needed them, and they have had an immense impact on my life. I emailed them to ask for prayer. I desired prayer over the situation in general, but specifically for Whitney. Though my email was short, I said to them, "It is so hard to be so far away when things like this happen. It is honestly hard to not be mad at God. I don't feel like I can be a brother to my sister right now." I believe God called me here. I believe I am right where God wants and needs me. I believe that I have been obedient to the call he has given me for the time being. I love being in Germany, but that does not mean it does not come without sacrifice and pain. Instances such as this only seem to magnify the pain. As a sinful being, my initial reaction is to throw a tantrum, shake my fist at God, and scream out, "Are you still paying attention? Do you understand the pain I am going through?"

Pain is not fun. Pain is not easy. Pain can be beneficial. We do not always know how, when, where, or why. Sometimes after time those questions become more visible. Other times they remain a mystery. Though my heart grows heavy, torn, burdened, and full of pain, I am reminded of God's faithfulness. There have been multiple situations where I have felt defeated, yet God showed up and worked wonders. At the end of the storm, I look back and smile as I see a few of the many ways in which God was at work, making it all worth it. Every heartache. Every pain. Every tear.

Lord, I do not claim to know everything. I do not understand all that is happening. I come before you with a heavy heart, a heart that is full of pain and sorrow. I want to be with my sister, and with my family. Yet you have a purpose for me here and now. Please help me to see that through the pain. Please do not allow this trial to distract me from the race I am running. Father, I believe that pain can be beneficial. Help me not to desire to be released from the pain so that I miss the lessons you have for me. May I not be too quick to see "the light at the end of the tunnel" that I neglect to meet with you right here, right now, in the midst of my pain. You never said it was going to be easy. You did say you are good. So I rest in your goodness. I rest in your loving arms. I take joy knowing you will never leave me nor forsake me. Amen.

MILE 16
DEDICATION

"We all have dreams. But in order to make dreams come into reality, it takes an awful lot of determination, dedication, self-discipline, and effort."
—Jesse Owens

"There will be days I don't know if I can do a marathon. There will be a lifetime knowing that I have."
—Unknown

"… and Nebuchadnezzar said to them: 'Is it true, Shadrach, Meshach, and Abednego, that you do not serve my gods or worship the image of gold I have set up? Now when you hear the sound of the horn, flute, zither, lyre, harp, pipe, and all kinds of music, if you are ready to fall down and worship the image I made, very good. But if you do not worship it, you will be thrown immediately into a blazing furnace. Then what god will be able to rescue you from my hand?'"
—Daniel 3:14-15

*T*HROUGHOUT THIS JOURNEY of writing I have occasionally encountered a few rough spots when I was unsure as to how I wanted to start a sentence, a paragraph, or a chapter. When hitting those rough spots, I found it beneficial to drop my notes, leave my desk, lace up my shoes, and go for an easy run. Putting my body and mind into a familiar pattern enables me to relax my heart and mind. Following a good, cleansing run, I am better prepared to tackle the task at hand. If, however, my schedule does not permit me to run on my favorite trail, I instead find a few friends and pick their brains, asking them questions without identifying why, hoping they can provide me with an inspirational springboard.

Facing that situation on this chapter, I asked some friends how they would define dedication, and what visual images the word brought to their minds. The responses were as diverse as were the images presented. Images varied from movies, such as *The Karate Kid* to *The Lord of The Rings*, to a lumberjack dripping with sweat as he chops a tree to provide his family with firewood, to Michelangelo meticulously brushing every stroke of the Sistine Chapel. What really struck me, though, was how each definition and each image described contained a character who was committed to a singular task. The lack of multiple commitments enabled the individual to exhibit the utmost dedication to his or her objective, not allowing any object to get in the way of his or her goal.

Below are some definitions of "dedication" given to me by some friends:

> "Something you stick to no matter what it is."
>
> "Focusing. Working hard, not giving up, focused on completing the task."
>
> "Going full-hearted."
>
> "Sticking to something or someone wholeheartedly even when things get rough."
>
> "Total commitment to someone or something."
>
> "A mindset where you are fixed on doing something, whatever it is you want to do, without giving up."

DEDICATION

Think about the numbers behind a marathon and you will get a better understanding of the amount of dedication required. A marathon is 26.2 miles, which is 138,435 feet. That 138,435 feet is 46,145 yards, or roughly the length of 461.5 football fields. The Empire State Building stands 1,454 feet tall, which means you could lay the building on its side 95 times and have yet to fully cover the distance of a marathon. The peak of Mt. Everest is 29,029 feet tall, or roughly the equivalent of one-fourth of a marathon.

The world record time for a marathon to date is 2 hours, 3 minutes, and 2 seconds.[57] To complete a marathon in this time requires a consistent mile pace of 4 minutes 41 seconds, which is 12 miles per hour. At that pace, in the time it would take you to watch an average-length movie (1 hour and 45 minutes), the runner will have completed slightly less than 22.5 miles. If you were to drive a steady 60 miles per hour in the time it took the fastest marathon to be run, you could safely travel from Los Angeles to San Diego (barring traffic). Most of us could not run one mile in less than five minutes, let alone maintain that kind of pace for 26.2 miles.

To successfully run a marathon, many experts recommend a training regimen that spans somewhere between sixteen and eighteen weeks (assuming you already have a base level of running fitness). The weeks of training can be as grueling and taxing as the race itself. With an eighteen-week training schedule, if you start on the opening day of the National Football League, you will finish during the playoffs. It is mind boggling to think that one can spend so much time training for one race.

I found a number of different eighteen-week training guides set up for runners of different abilities. One training guide has the runner compiling 435 miles over the eighteen weeks, or roughly 4.8 miles per day. The next level increases the total mileage to 466 miles, a daily average of 5.7. A more advanced training regimen calls for 620 miles, bumping the daily average up to 6.8 miles. For those who are visual learners, the distance between Paris and Madrid is roughly 650 miles.

Training for, and then completing, a marathon takes dedication. As defined by my friends, dedication refers to someone who is fully committed to something or someone with an attitude that refuses to give up regardless of the difficulty. The dedication of a runner will not only be tested on the actual day of the race but in the many weeks of training. Commitment is needed, not only to follow certain things, like your training plan, but also to refrain from things that will inhibit your training and racing performance. By cultivating a spirit of determination early and often throughout your training, you will reap the benefits not only during Mile 16 but throughout the entire race.

While the training regimen requires much dedication, there are a few things that can be instituted to assist you along the way, perhaps none more important than finding a training partner. Admittedly, there are days when running is the last thing you will want to do. You are busy. Your legs are heavy. The weather is less than ideal. Yet if you can find someone to train with, that accountability will make things easier on days when the list of reasons not to run is longer than the run itself.

I have found that in training (in running but also in team sports) you create a sense of community. A result of this community is the concept that you are not only letting yourself down by choosing not to run, you are also letting down your teammate/running partner. Accountability is achieved (whether directly spoken about or not), which proves to be extremely beneficial. Additionally, it helps to have someone you can talk to who can relate to what you are going through while you train.

While in Germany I have been blessed to have two friends, Dreves and Jim, who have held me accountable in my marathon training. Both are experienced marathon runners and were eager to listen, encourage, celebrate, and challenge me. Unfortunately Dreves is in the United States and was unable to participate with me, but he constantly answered emails and checked up on my training progress. Jim walked side-by-side with me (quite literally as I ran my third marathon) and was a huge encouragement and blessing. He is an eternal optimist, so regardless of how poorly I felt, or how far off my goal I was, he found a way to encourage me and put a smile on my face.

DEDICATION

The night after running my slowest marathon, Jim sent me an email that I will never forget. He had put together a tremendous "pit crew" to tag along and cheer me on at the race. That night I was depleted and discouraged. In his email he spoke encouraging words and affirmed that he was proud of me. Those words were priceless to me, and they carried so much weight because they came from a man who had walked the journey with me.

Another aspect of accountability that has proven to be immensely beneficial for me has been keeping a running journal. Following training runs, I come back and make a few quick notes about the run. Some days I write more than others, and some days I forget to write anything at all. But it has proven invaluable. I make sure to write down the distance I ran and the time in which I ran it. To help me remember the run, I sometimes write about the weather, or some train of thought I had dancing through my mind during the run. I find it helpful to include how I felt during the run. Were my legs heavy and sluggish? Did my lungs have a hard time keeping up with the pace? Did I just come from a frustrating meeting, where I was trying to run away from an issue and blow off steam? If I found a food or a time of day that really bode well (or didn't!), I wrote it down and knew what I needed to try again or avoid.

My running journal also reminds me of my progress. Late in the stages of training, it was encouraging to look back and read that my first double-digit training run was "… tough, frustrating, difficult. I wanted to quit. My legs couldn't make it up the last hill. My mind was not strong and was willing to give in to my body's demands …"[58] This compared to an entry about a twenty-one-mile run being "… tough but doable. Legs were strong in the end, my mind stayed focused. Only five more to the finish line? I can do it. I feel ready."[59]

Yes, there are going to be good days and bad days while training. Recently as is his custom, my dad gave me some simple yet profound wisdom. His recent words were timely as he said, "Take the good with the bad. For all the practices where you walk away wanting to quit, there are going to be just as many reminding you of why you're there." Allow your running journal to serve as a reminder of where you have come and where you are headed.

While there will be visible signs of what you do during training that reflect dedication, there are also things that you don't do that require just as much dedication, and for each person it will differ. Despite some of the differences, a cost to virtually every marathon runner will be time and energy. Regardless of your pace, running takes time. And it is not just the time spent running. It takes time to get to your running trail, whether that be in a local park or the local gym. It takes time to recover from a run. It takes time to plan your run. It requires dedication to find daily time within your schedule to fit in the required runs.

While running can be very rejuvenating, it can also be draining. Running gives me an opportunity to rejuvenate mentally and emotionally. I simply wish I could do so without taking such a heavy tax on my body! During training there will be events or opportunities that will have to be turned down. For example, if you have planned to get your long run taken care of early Saturday morning, a late evening out with friends on Friday night might not be the best idea. By saying yes to running a marathon and all it entails, there will be many things you will say no to.

Though there are numerous examples of reasons why running a marathon takes dedication, the following is one that I find a little humorous. It takes dedication to be willing to take energy supplements while running. Goo gels are the supplement I, and probably most marathon runners, choose to use. There are many different brands, and there are a variety of flavors. I am a believer in the products and think they are helpful for running long distances. However, to me they taste disgusting. I have been adventurous and tried the many different brands and different flavors. There are some that taste better than others, but there is just something about the consistency and smell that instantly grosses me out. During my training runs as well as the actual marathons, I grimace every time I pull one out. I contemplate not swallowing it but I start to think about what it will do for me and for my body. Knowing it will provide my body with needed nutrients, I tough it out and let

DEDICATION

the goo gel do its job. With every drop that goes into my mouth, I am reminded that I am dedicated to the race. I focus on my goal and realize this is a necessary step in order to achieve that goal.

Marathons require dedication to our training. In a similar way, when we move into a personal relationship with Jesus Christ, he asks for us to be dedicated to him. God wants our focus. The type of dedication required is not half-hearted dedication that only remains loyal when things are going well. Dedication is being committed through the good and bad. Our dedication to God can be seen in how we trust him. By looking at the lives of Shadrach, Meshach, and Abednego, we will see servants of God who showed their dedication through their trust and commitment to God, regardless of the circumstances.

We first get a glimpse of these men in the first chapter of the book of Daniel. Nebuchadnezzar had come into Jerusalem and destroyed it. The majority of the people were left for dead. The Temple was pillaged. Their way of life was completely and utterly destroyed. A few men were carried off to be assimilated into the Babylonian lifestyle. These men were supposed to be "the best of the best." They were handsome, physically fit, educated, quick learners, and fit for the king's palace. Among those mentioned were Daniel, Shadrach, Meshach, and Abednego. They were taken captive and for three years underwent a sort of brainwashing program. They were to be stripped of their Jewish way of life and conform to the Babylonian lifestyle.

The first step in morphing these Jewish men into Babylonians was to change their names. The original names of these three men were Hananiah, Mishael, and Azariah. These three Jewish names reminded them of the God the Jews worshiped. The names Shadrach, Meshach, and Abednego paid homage to the Babylonian gods. As they stepped into a foreign land, every time they heard their new names mentioned, they were reminded they were in a hostile place that was striving to strip them of their former way of life. For three years they were under scrutiny and daily challenged to adopt to a new way of living and a new belief system.

We are often too quick to look at the "home-run" and neglect to see all the preparation that brought the athlete to that point. Many people look at the day of the marathon and are impressed with what you accomplished on that specific day, without taking into account the months of training that brought you to the starting line. In the same way, we should not look at Shadrach, Meshach, and Abednego in the fiery furnace without taking into account the three years they spent in training. Those three years were not easy. They were difficult, hard, pressing, and frustrating. Those three years of difficulty prepared them and set them up for a great victory further down the road. In the same way, do not be too quick to wish your difficult days away. Do not fail to realize that in those trials God may be preparing you for something great.

During those three years, Shadrach, Meshach, and Abednego were able to fully solidify their dedication to the one true Lord. They were likely challenged in many ways. The way in which they were educated was altered. Their daily diets were modified. The language they were supposed to speak changed. Their names were different. While we do not know much detail about these three years, I believe their dedication to God was extraordinary.

As they were going through these classes and rituals to assimilate into the Babylonian lifestyle, I wonder how many times they were ridiculed for their beliefs. The guards probably rubbed in the fact that their temple had just been destroyed and their wives and children murdered. The guards likely mocked God by saying, "Why didn't your god protect you when we came to fight?" or "You have been here three years and your god still hasn't rescued you … has he forgotten you?" During these years there were plenty of opportunities for these three men to abandon God. Times when they could have relieved the pressure, the abuse, and the antagonism—if only they would have denied their faith. But they did not. They were dedicated. Throughout these three years these men proved their dedication among their circle of influence. And after three years of witnessing to their circle, they were given an opportunity to display their dedication to the entire nation.

DEDICATION

Shadrach, Meshach, and Abednego displayed their dedication to the Lord in front of the entire nation by acting differently. King Nebuchadnezzar had summoned the people to come to the grand unveiling of his newly-constructed image. The structure measured ninety feet tall and nine feet wide. It was not mediocre. It was massive! Nebuchadnezzar wanted to display his power by revealing such a large image to his kingdom. With that in mind, he ordered the satraps, prefects, governors, advisers, treasurers, judges, magistrates, and all other provincial officials to attend the special celebration. Music and dancing were also on the agenda. But the real purpose of the celebration was to require the people to bow down and worship the image that Nebuchadnezzar had erected.

I suspect that there were many people huddled together in the Babylonian city center, eager to see the unveiling of the structure, likely kept hidden by a massive curtain. Thousands of Babylonians were waiting for the signal to bow down. Some would do it out of fear and reverence of the Babylonian gods; others because of fear of Nebuchadnezzar. After all, everyone knew what would happen to them if they failed to bow down. The heat of the furnace and the thought of burning alive was strong enough to convince those unsure about bowing down.

As I envision the scene, I hear the music blaring while the curtain falls and thousands of people fall to their knees. About halfway between the image and the end of the crowd stands Abednego. He refuses to bow down to a false god. Those directly beside him notice he is not kneeling and urge him to kneel. They remind him of the punishment he will face. Their focus is no longer on the massive golden image, but on the legs of a man who is still standing. Farther behind him and off to the right stands Shadrach. His palms are sweating, for he knows the statement he just made. Yet as he raises his head, he looks off in the distance and sees Abednego. For a moment their eyes meet and their hearts are united. A look back over his left shoulder and Shadrach can see Meshach standing tall as well. The music is still playing. The thousands are still worshiping. But these three men are still standing. Three men among a sea of people. Three men unwilling to compromise their beliefs and unwilling to deny their God.

I wonder if there were any other Jews in the crowd who had been taken captive three years prior along with Daniel, Shadrach, Meshach, and Abednego? Those are the only names written in the text, but were there others who were taken captive and over the three years failed to remain dedicated to the one true God? If so, and I believe there were, what do you think was going through their minds and hearts when they saw these three men refuse to kneel? Some probably mocked them. They were among the Babylonians who sneered at them and reminded them of the grueling punishment that was reserved for them. They had come from a lineage that embraced fickleness. Being captured by Nebuchadnezzar provided yet another opportunity to shift allegiance.

However, I also think there were those who knelt but in hindsight wished they had not. There were those who believed in the same God as these three men, yet they knelt down out of fear and self-preservation. The dedication of Shadrach, Meshach, and Abednego influenced not just those who held different beliefs, but those who had the same beliefs. After seeing Shadrach, Meshach, and Abednego refuse to kneel, hopefully there were some who paused and questioned whether there was anything in their lives to which they had as much dedication. Some who knelt may have questioned where along the line they had they lost their dedication, and how they could go about getting it back.

King Nebuchadnezzar had planned an extravagant ceremony in which to reveal his new statue. Despite all the people, all the music, and all the hype, people walked away not talking about a massive gold image, but about three young men who refused to kneel down.

Their decision did not please Nebuchadnezzar. His grand plan for revealing his newly-created image was ruined by three men who refused to be intimidated. Nebuchadnezzar summoned them to his presence with the hope of finding out the rationale behind their decision, and this provided them yet another opportunity to display their dedication to God.

DEDICATION

With these three men in front of him, Nebuchadnezzar spelled things out one last time, just in case they did not clearly understand. He rephrased what they were supposed to do when they heard the music. He reiterated what would happen to them if they once again refused. But Shadrach, Meshach, and Abednego were fully aware of what was ahead of them if they refused to kneel down. So often we fail to stand up for God because we play the "what if" card. "What if my boss fires me because I won't compromise my morals?" "What if my roommate makes fun of me because I read my Bible?" "What if my friends no longer want to hang out with me?" We allow ourselves to play the "what if" game, and we are filled with fear. For these guys the answer to the question, "What if we don't bow down" was laid plain and simple for them—"You will be thrown in the blazing furnace."

Fully aware of the consequences, they once again refused to kneel. Their hearts were full of trust in their God. Their response is recorded:

> O Nebuchadnezzar, we do not need to defend ourselves before you in this matter. If we are thrown into the blazing furnace, the God we serve is able to save us from it, and he will rescue us from your hand, O king. But even if he does not, we want you to know, O king, that we will not serve your gods or worship the image of gold you have set up.[60]

Their trust in God is fully evident when they claim, "He is able to save us." They trusted that God would protect and deliver them from Nebuchadnezzar's hand. I can hear them saying, "Either our God will rescue us from the fire, or we will die in the fire. Either way we will be delivered from your hand." For them it is a win-win situation. They trusted their God. They were dedicated to their God. In the end, they were delivered by their God. "They trusted in him [God] and defiled the king's command and were willing to give up their lives rather than serve or worship any god except their own God."[61] Their three years of dedication to God prior to this event prepared them for this day.

Running your race requires your dedication. You will need to be focused. Work hard. Refuse to give up. Your race will require you to be totally committed. May the same be said of your dedication to the Lord. May you stick with it, even when things start to get rough. May those who witness you repeat the words of Nebuchadnezzar, testifying that you trusted in God and gave up your life rather than serving or worshiping any other god.

Father, thank you for the example in your word of Shadrach, Meshach, and Abednago. They are examples to us of those who were fully dedicated. Father, may the same be said of us. May you empower us and give us steadfast hearts that are unwilling to give in to temptations. May you surround us with men and women with hearts after your own. Your Holy Spirit has come to us so that we might not be timid or scared. Father, may we not kneel to worthless idols, but stand tall, strong, and dedicated to you. Amen.

MILE 17
WORSHIP

"I believe God made me for a purpose, but he also made me fast. And when I run, I feel his pleasure."
—Eric Liddell

"Do not flatter yourselves: if you go to places of worship merely to look about you or to hear music,
you are not worshipping God."
—Charles H. Spurgeon

"On the third day Abraham looked up and saw the place in the distance. He said to his servants, 'Stay here with the donkey while I and the boy go over there. We will worship, and then we will come back to you.'"
—Genesis 22:4-5

ALLOW ME TO let you in on a little secret. I am a terrible singer. The cliché phrase, "He couldn't carry a tune in a bucket," is an understatement of the horrid noise my vocal chords produce in an attempt to sing. If you don't believe me, ask anyone who has sat within two rows of me at a worship service or anyone who has received a singing voicemail from me. If they have an actual test to gauge whether someone is tone deaf, I know for a fact I would pass the test with ease. Added to my horrible singing skill, or pure lack of skill, I have no rhythm. When those around me start clapping *as well as* singing, something inside of me cringes with fear and embarrassment. I am always left with a difficult choice—do I clap or do I sing? Clapping *and* singing at the same time is simply not an option for me. If I attempt to do both, either I will fall off beat (assuming I actually started on beat) or I will start singing words that are nowhere to be found in the lyrics of the song.

Here is the ironic thing—I love to sing. I love singing in church. I enjoy singing while running. I love to sing along to the radio. When I cook, there is nothing better than turning up the music volume and letting loose in the kitchen. Singing provides me, and usually those around me, with enjoyment and entertainment. I can never tell if others are laughing with me or at me. It really does not matter, because I will continue to sing anyway.

For a while my lack of singing ability wore me down spiritually. It didn't happen suddenly, but was a gradual slide that made me feel further and further away from God. Why? Somewhere along the line I had come up with a skewed and incorrect definition of "worship." I used to think that worship was primarily composed of singing songs to God.

This incorrect perception of worship made me afraid that I was unable to properly and acceptably worship God. After all, I knew how poor a singer I was, and if that was the way in which Christians worshiped God, then I must have been extremely far away from God. The truth behind it might not be accurate, but as a young child it seemed logical to me. I couldn't sing well, therefore I couldn't worship very well.

WORSHIP

Eventually, it was a song that helped begin the transformation of my mind and heart on this issue. The song "I Love You, Lord" helped reconstruct my perception of worship from one solely based on singing to one that is more biblically accurate. Everything we do as Christians should be an act of worship of God. Within the song are the lyrics, "I love you, Lord, and I lift my voice. To worship you, Oh my soul rejoice! Take joy, my King, in what you hear. May it be a sweet, sweet sound in your ear."

Offering these words up as a prayer to God enabled him to work in my heart. The words "Take joy, my King, in what you hear …" refreshed my heart unimaginably. The concept that my voice was bringing God joy, regardless of what I sounded like to others, lifted a huge weight off my shoulders. The closing words, "May it be a sweet, sweet sound in your ear," enabled me to realize that God was not worried about the sound my voice was creating, but the intention of my heart.

In addition to this song, the story in Genesis of Abraham helped me understand a more complete definition of worship. In Genesis 22, God asks Abraham to sacrifice his son, Isaac. So Abraham puts together a small caravan of individuals and when he sees the spot for sacrificing Isaac off in the distance, he instructs everyone with him to "stay here with the donkey while I and the boy go over there. We will worship and then we will come back to you."[62] While the entire story of Abraham's faithfulness and trust is phenomenal, there are three words that jump out at me: "We will worship."

We are not given the precise details of what they brought with them, but I don't see anything in the text that suggests Abraham had a donkey carrying musical instruments. Isaac was carrying wood and rope, not a hymnal. These two individuals went off to worship, and there is no definitive evidence they worshiped by singing. Don't get me wrong, singing definitely could have been a part of what they did, but it was not the *only* way they worshiped. Abraham and Isaac ventured up the mountain to worship through obedience, action, thought, and the way in which they lived their lives. Singing can be a part of worship, but it is not the only way to worship. In everything we do we have the opportunity to worship God.

In regard to the story of Abraham, the word *shachah* is used in the original language to define the worship of Abraham and Isaac. This particular word is the most common word used for worship in the Old Testament. A translation of the word is "to bow down, to prostrate, to fall flat." By the definition and the imagery attached, it is expressing the knowledge of the Lordship of God within our life. By falling prostrate before God, by falling flat, we are humbling ourselves and considering ourselves nothing before a holy God.

Looking back at Mile 16 and our discussion of Shadrach, Meshach, and Abednego, *shachah* was the same type of worship they were asked to exert toward Nebuchadnezzar's golden image. They were commanded to fall flat and proclaim that the image had lordship in their lives (and they refused).

The word *abad* is also used in Scripture to describe worship. This word can be seen in the second chapter of Genesis, where it refers to worship as working. Adam and Eve were created to work within the Garden of Eden. The garden was not a place in which they kicked their feet up, took long naps in a hammock while sipping on fruity drinks, and watched the sunset. They had tasks to perform while in the garden. There was work to accomplish. Through this work, and through their efforts, they were worshiping God. The work we do can be a service and can be worship. Thus, worship is not simply limited to what we do on a given Sunday morning. It is not limited to singing. Worship should infiltrate our daily lives.

In the New Testament there is another word for worship, *sebomai*. This finds its origins in the seventh chapter of Mark's Gospel. Here Jesus answers the Pharisees as he quotes Isaiah, "These people honor me with their lips, but their hearts are far from me. They worship me in vain; their teachings are but rules taught by men."[63] The word *sebomai* refers to those who revere, adore; those who are devout. With Jesus' criticism of the Pharisees, he is stating that the worship given to him by their actions does not reflect one who adores and is devoted to him. Jesus is implying that through the very way in which we live we are (or are not) worshiping God.

WORSHIP

From looking at Scripture, we can see that worship is not solely limited to singing. Rather, worship is an attitude of humility, reverence, and adoration that is reflected by the way in which we work and live our lives. Our lives should be lives of worship. We do not have events where we "come and worship." We should live lives where we are constantly worshiping. On Sunday mornings, worship should not stop when the music ends; it should continue through adoration, fellowship, sacrificing, teaching, working, etc. Worship is not an act; it is a lifestyle.

Unfortunately, I have not always had this attitude and understanding of worship. It has been a long process, but throughout the years there have been monumental moments that have guided me toward a better understanding of worship—one of which I would like to share with you as it relates to worshiping through athletics.

Once when I was twelve years old, my dad and I traveled to Illinois for an overnight soccer trip. I was playing on a traveling team and we had one of our first tournaments out of state. It was an exhilarating weekend full of fun and new experiences. One of the new experiences was having a soccer game on a Sunday morning. On the car ride to the field, my dad and I were discussing the fact we were missing church. At one point in the conversation he asked me, "Have you ever thought about praying before playing?" As always (even to this day), a way to get my attention was to reference the Green Bay Packers. Knowing this, my dad added, "You know how when the Packers score a touchdown you will sometimes see the guy go on one knee, or point to the sky. Now I'm not necessarily talking about doing that, but you can worship while you play soccer." Those final words struck me—worship while you play soccer. Five small words that drastically transformed my viewpoint of worship. It wasn't an instantaneous thing—I did not go out that day and have answers to all my questions. But it proved to be an idea that, over years, snowballed into something bigger.

Sometime after that weekend I was in church when the congregation sang the song, "Take My Life and Let It Be." As was the case with "I Love You, Lord," a few words struck my heart and make me smile every time I pray them,

> Take my life, and let it be consecrated, Lord, to Thee.
> Take my moments and my days; let them flow in ceaseless praise.
> Take my hands, and let them move at the impulse of Thy love.
> Take my feet, and let them be swift and beautiful for Thee.

The last line in that song has proven monumental for me. Soccer, as well as running, are activities that are all about what your feet can do. How fast they can move; how long they can carry you; how quickly and accurately they can control a ball. The sports I love to participate in directly deal with my feet. Singing a prayer that my feet would be swift and beautiful for Jesus helped me realize that in everything I do I can worship God. In the same way I would sing and pray that my voice would be a sweet sound in Jesus' ears. I was singing and praying that my feet would do beautiful things for him.

With this in mind I began to see the soccer field as a place where I could worship. I understand that I was not gifted with musical ability. However, God did give me an ability to run and an ability to play soccer. With that gift, it is my joy and privilege to give that back to God. The Lord cares for me, loves me, and is omniscient, aware of all I do. Knowing this, I desire to be a blessing to God by the way in which I play. Through the attitude of my heart, the words that come out of my mouth, and the way I treat my teammates, referees and opposition, all of those become ways in which I can serve God. If my voice can be a sweet sound, I want my performance as a player to be a sweet sight for Jesus.

If you were to paint a mental image of a guy relaxing and watching sports, what would it look like? I picture a man sitting in a very comfortable chair. His feet are propped up. He has a blanket on him to stay warm. The remote control is in his hand so he can perfectly execute remote control management. There are snacks surrounding him, keeping his taste buds dancing and his stomach content. All of this adds up and you see the man sitting there with a smile of contentment on his face. It is a beautiful thing.

Prior to soccer games in high school and college, I would attempt to get my heart in the right position so that God could

WORSHIP

relax and enjoy watching me play. It was my desire to put a smile on God's face while I played, and to bless and worship him through my actions on the field. Prior to every game in college I took a few minutes to warm up by myself. I didn't want anyone else around me. I didn't want to be seen or bothered. Taking my dad's advice, I would take that as an opportunity to pray and offer up my work and effort as worship to the Lord.

While running, my customary warm-up routine involves quietly singing a prayer:

> Here I am to worship. Here I am to bow down. Here I am to say that you're my God. You're all together lovely, altogether worthy, altogether wonderful to me. So here I am to worship. Here I am to bow down. Here I am to say that you're my God.

The words "Here I am to worship" are repeated over and over again because my worship cannot be contained by singing; my worship for my God is through everything I do. This has been the same for running, and I have been blessed to have witnessed others worshiping while they run.

One of the greatest benefits of running outside is being able to see the beauty that surrounds you while you run. Having lived in fairly rural areas, I have been able to run on many soft trails, providing beautiful views. While in high school every now and then I would bike down to the ocean and go for a run in the sand. My favorite trail in New Hampshire has a brilliant combination of little hills, shaded spots, sunny stretches, woods, views of the water, and unique terrain as you jog over rustic bridges made of fallen trees. I have run this trail so many times that I actually have a favorite step of the run. There is one point in the run where I am just filled with energy and awe.

By running we are able to step into the world God created and enjoy his beauty. When our hearts are moved by the beauty of a trail, or when our breath is taken away by the multi-colored leaves gently falling from the trees as a gentle fall breeze crosses our face, acknowledging that God created it all and enjoying his creation is an act of worship. He is pleased as we enjoy what he has created.

Recently I had the privilege of running with a great friend, Jim. He took me on a run that has helped me worship God while running by admiring his creation. One day he took me out on his favorite trail in Germany. He described the trail as a poem. It starts off with a grueling bang as you charge uphill. Jim explained how at first he found it difficult to make it up the hill when his eyes were fixed down at the ground. Only after he fixed his eyes upward was he able to conquer the hill. As you reach the hill's crest, you slowly start to descend. The trees are still heavily covering the trail, so it is dark and you could possibly lose your way. Soon enough your pace starts to pick up. Something within you realizes the hard part is over and there is nothing but good ahead. At precisely that moment, as you look down the path, you can see the end of the trail. The trees are still covering the trail, but they form a beautiful window, letting in light from the outside. You know that once you hit that light, you have reached your destination. With every step the window grows as you see more and more light; inside there is a growing anticipation of getting to the other side. As you reach the other side you realize you are home.

Another friend of mine also worships while running, though it is different from Jim. She uses running as a time to talk to God. Stephanie was my training partner for a marathon we both ran. Throughout training we ran once or twice a week together, mainly the long runs. The morning of our race we traveled down together and as we were getting ourselves ready I noticed something that at first seemed a little strange to me. On the day of a race it is not uncommon to see runners wrap a wristband or tape on their arm with their desired splits. I am one of those runners, so as I was getting mine situated on my arm I glanced over at Stephanie and noticed her doing the same, though something didn't quite look right. Previously we had talked about our individual paces and concluded that we would be running at different splits the day of the race. However, her wristband did not have any times at all. Confused, I discretely tried to get another look. After getting a closer look I did not see forty-two different times (we were running in

WORSHIP

Europe so the marathon was in kilometers, not miles—a marathon is 26.2 miles, or 42 kilometers), but forty-two different names.

Prior to the race Stephanie had decided that during each kilometer in the race she ran, she would pray for a specific person. Her marathon was a race marked by prayers. With every step she took she was connecting with the Lord and offering up family and friends before the throne of God. With yet another look (and perhaps by this time I had lost my ability to be discrete) I noticed there were specific requests next to each name. I noticed there were students written on her wrist whom she considered as daughters. There were friends she considered family. Her marathon was a time in which she could go out and have hours of uninterrupted prayer time with God. She ran extremely well, and while I know her friends who watched were proud of what she accomplished, I am certain her heavenly Father was proud of the way she worshiped while running.

Worship is our heart's response to God. We should not limit our worship to church. We are the church, and we are a worshiping people. Worship incorporates all aspects of our lives, including running. Use the Mile 17 marker as a worship reminder. As you run, worship. As you worship, run.

Father, thank you for the examples that you have provided to us, especially the men and women who follow you with all their hearts who are working together to encourage and inspire one another. Thank you for the example of Abraham and the way in which he worshiped you. Thank you for the many individuals within our lives who have helped us better understand what it means to worship. Father, we ask that our lives would be lives defined by worship. Amen.

MILE 18
ANTICIPATION

"Obstacles are what you see when you
take your eyes off the goal."
—Luis Escobar

"But our citizenship is in heaven. And we eagerly await a
Savior from there, the Lord Jesus Christ."
—Philippians 3:20

AS MY LEGS carried me past the sign for Mile 18, something inside of me changed. I suddenly had a renewed sense of enthusiasm. I felt a previously untapped resource of energy and determination. I knew it was not the weather, as I had just run out of tree coverage and was now in the middle of the street with the sun glaring down on my every step. It certainly was not the terrain. The course's greatest incline was still a few miles away, and Mile 18 marked the start of a slow, grueling, gradual incline.

My excitement was rooted in the knowledge I had friends who were coming to see me run, and they were scattered on the sidelines somewhere between Miles 18 and 22. In the days prior to the race we had mapped out the ideal places for them to stand, so I was expecting them and looking forward to seeing them. In previous miles, I had been spurred on by spectators—they handed me water, clapped as I ran by, and cheered my name. Yet this was a small taste of what was waiting for me. While I loved hearing my name being cheered (especially with all the foreign accents), the previous cheers would not compare to the ones coming from people I knew, friends of mine who were there to spur me on.

With every step, I knew I was getting closer to my friends, whose voices I would recognize and whose words I would not have to translate. Every incline I climbed, every turn I made, I ran with anticipation, hoping I would see them at the top of the hill or around the corner as I made my next turn. I anticipated their support, and it exhilarated me. In so doing, I realized how one of the many feelings racing through my mind and heart was a spirit of anticipation. I had an advanced realization, a foretaste, something I was expecting and eagerly looking forward to. While this was dominating my thoughts throughout Mile 18, I soon realized there had been a lot of anticipation throughout the race itself.

I had spent months preparing for the race. I thought I had done everything I needed to do. Yet despite my greatest efforts to prepare, there were definitely moments of difficulty throughout the race itself. Whenever I hit one of those rough patches, I forced myself to choose the next tangible milestone I needed to reach. Early in the race, I was looking forward to being a quarter of the

ANTICIPATION

way done. After hitting that benchmark my targets became a little less daunting. Rather than map out another 6.5 mile chunk, which would land me at the halfway point, I broke it down into two separate three-mile segments. Once I hit the next marker, I gave myself a new goal, and then another, and then another, and so on.

I needed something to look forward to, something that I was aiming for. Knowing each step was taking me closer to my goal, each step had purpose, power, and energy. When I would stop at a water station to drink some water and eat a banana, the next water station served as my next marker. As I ran away from one water station, I was running toward the next. Within me the anticipation grew. Obviously my ultimate destination, and goal, was to cross the finish line. Yet, sometimes throughout the race I could not form a vision of the finish line. There were too many miles and obstacles standing in my way. However, I knew that the next water station brought me one more water station closer to the finish line.

While running, I also had a growing expectation of the three most feared words in marathon running: "hitting the wall." Within most marathon training programs, your longest run generally does not exceed twenty-one or twenty-two miles. Of course, that is at least four miles short of the finish line. Somewhere within those four miles you can (gulp) hit a wall. It is not something that is necessarily looked forward to with joy; frustration and pain mar most people's feelings about the wall. Cramps, weariness, headaches, heavy legs, and perhaps vomiting are characteristics of the wall. It is not fun, but it is something anticipated.

During my very first marathon I had heard horror stories about "the wall." It seemed as though everyone was constantly saying, "It is not a matter of IF you hit the wall, it is a matter of WHEN you hit the wall." Young, inexperienced, full of hubris, I shot out of the gate thinking there was no way *I* was going to hit the wall. Without patience or much of a strategy, I blazed through the first 13.1 miles in under ninety minutes. I felt good, I felt energetic, and I felt young. Miles 13-20 were actually much of the same. Then it came, and when it came it hit me like a semi-truck. Somewhere between Miles 20 and 21 I flat out hit the wall. First my right hamstring cramped, then my left hamstring. My calves were jealous of the attention my hamstrings were getting, so soon after they decided if they were to cramp up too, I would pay attention to them. It took me under ninety minutes to run 13.1 miles. It took me close to seventy minutes to finish my final six miles. The wall cannot be fully described. It can only be fully experienced.

Despite the ugliness of the wall there is at least one other thing you should anticipate while running … the finish line. Do we not all share the goal of crossing the line and finishing the race? We long for that moment where we hear the music from a few blocks away. You can hear the roar of the crowd cheering as each runner breaches the horizon and comes into sight. Months of training, hundreds of miles, and thousands of drops of sweat are all about to pay off as that beautiful finish line comes into view. Your journey has brought you more than 130,000 feet and you are right there. So close you can see it. So close you can hear it. Something deep inside of you longs to finish, longs to make it across that line. You had a small taste of water along the way, but soon you will enjoy the most refreshing glass of water ever to quench your thirst. You have received cheers along the way, yet it was a slight impression of the cheers you will receive as you cross the line. You anticipate the end of the race, and your great longing to do so spurs you on. Cramping muscles, parched throats, and heavy legs all fail to stop you as your sights are focused on finishing what you have started.

Do we anticipate heaven in the same way we anticipate finishing a marathon? Is there a longing and a hope deep inside of us that is ready to cross the line into eternity? What do you anticipate as far as your relationship with Jesus is concerned? Is there any advanced realization of what is to come? How often do we arrive at church with the expectation of encountering God? How does our eternal anticipation affect the way we live our lives? Even if the earthly finish line seems in the far-off distance, our view of eternity should impact every step of the way. That anticipation should spur us on, encourage us, and give us hope when the evil one attacks.

Lambs among wolves. Valleys in the shadow of death. Carrying a cross of self-denial. Leaving everything behind. Persecution.

ANTICIPATION

Hardships. Temptation. All are anticipated aspects of the Christian walk. Jesus did not say to his disciples, "Follow me. It will be easy, it will be carefree, and it will not be hard at all." In fact, Jesus constantly reminded his disciples of the exact opposite. There is a cost to discipleship. Therefore, as followers of Jesus Christ we should anticipate difficulties, trials, hardships, and frustrations.

Some of the difficulties we face are beyond our control, but some of them are a result of who we are and what is inside of us. We are imperfect people living in an imperfect world. War, famine, disease, and hatred fill our world. I recently came across a witty remark stating, "The evening news is where they start by saying 'good evening' and then proceeding to tell you everything going on in the world that makes it far from good." Such is the world in which we live.

This is not simply the world in which we presently live, but the way it has been since the fall of man. I once heard the following quote but unfortunately cannot remember where it came from. If I could give credit to whoever penned it, I would do so in a heartbeat. These words have pounded in my heart time and time again. The author wrote, "For those who belong to the Kingdom of God, living on Earth is the closest they will ever come to hell. For those who do not belong to the Kingdom of God, living on Earth is the closest they will ever come to heaven."

For those who believe in the Kingdom of God, they have something else to look forward to—there is a place called heaven that holds our hope and anticipation. Paul, as he wrote to the church in Philippi, reminds us that

> … our citizenship is in heaven. And we eagerly await a Savior from there, the Lord Jesus Christ, who, by the power that enables him to bring everything under his control, will transform our lowly bodies so that they will be like his glorious body.[64]

Eagerly. What a beautiful word that is. Paul is describing an intense longing, a strong desire, and a great earnestness, deep inside of him to cross the finish line and find his eternal resting place.

In a different letter to Timothy, Paul describes his longing for Jesus' appearing as he finishes his earthly race. Paul knows he has run his race with perseverance, and in such a way that he will be called a child of God.[65] Paul expressed his anticipation for heaven in the same way I looked forward to seeing my friends scattered on the sideline between Miles 18 and 22, although Paul's anticipation was far grander and more magnificent. As Paul was readying to cross into eternity, he was overcome with a source of energy and enthusiasm. He knew he was about to see the heroes of the Bible. Soon he would be swapping stories with Moses, David, Daniel, and Esther.

While running we can be motivated by those who are cheering for us and calling us by name. It is one thing to hear cheers. It is another to hear your name cheered. It will be one thing to hear humans call your name, and a different thing altogether to hear God call you by name and welcome you in as his child. You can imagine the sound of spectators cheering as you cross the finish line of your race. Yet can you imagine the sound of angels rejoicing in heaven when your name is written in the Book of Life?

There will be obstacles in the way. There will be tough times ahead that will blur our vision. There will be bumps and bruises. Times when you cramp up, fall down, feel defeated. However, deep inside of you there is a longing, a great eagerness, an anticipation of what is yet to come—the day when you will cross the line and be in Jesus' presence forever.

While I think about the hope and longing we as disciples of Jesus Christ have, I recognize there may be some reading these words who do not claim to follow Jesus. You have not made a decision to commit your life to Christ. Perhaps you still cannot wrap your head around the idea. Maybe you have never heard of Jesus before and do not know how to begin a relationship with him. Whatever your current situation, if you are desiring to begin a relationship with Jesus Christ, I encourage you to do so now.

If the Lord is standing at the door to your heart and knocking, he is waiting for you to answer.[66] In order to open the door we must realize that we are sinners; we have strayed from the path God laid

ANTICIPATION

out for us. As sinners we have fallen short of the glory of God.[67] Our disobedience creates a separation between us and God. We, on our own, are not worthy nor are we capable of bridging the gap of separation. Yet while we were still sinners Christ died for us.[68] Jesus claims (and is) the only way, the only truth, and the life.[69]

To give Jesus control of our lives, we must come to him and admit that we are sinners. We must repent of and flee from our wicked ways. To repent means to make a 180-degree turn. While in the past we were going one way, we must now turn around and go the exact opposite direction. We were headed toward death, and are now headed toward life. We must repent of our unbelief. Previously, there was an unwillingness to accept who Jesus was and what he did. The heart must repent and believe that God loved the world so much that he gave his one and only Son.[70]

If you are reading these words and have never asked God to inhabit you and take control of your life, I encourage you to do so now. You may talk to God about whatever is on your mind and heart. If you are unsure of what to say I invite you to pray these words:

> Father, I know that I am a sinner. I have strayed from the path you have asked me to walk. To this point my life has been my own. Jesus, I ask that you would forgive me. I ask that you would come into my heart and into my life to take control. I believe that you came to this earth and lived a perfect life, yet still went to the cross to pay the penalty of sin for the whole world. My sin sent you to the cross, and you paid the debt that I cannot pay. You defeated death, were raised to life, and are now in heaven. For that, I want to give you my life. I want to follow you. Lord, I anticipate you coming again, so that I may spend eternity with you.

Can I ask you to do me a favor? If you just prayed that prayer for the first time, tell someone. Additionally, find someone who will walk with you and disciple you as you begin your new journey.

If you did not pray that prayer because you are already a child of God, can you do me a favor? Can you pray for those who may have prayed that prayer for the first time? Go before the throne of God on their behalf and pray for them. Rejoice with them and praise

God that another child has been added to the family. Also pray that they would be able to find a mentor, a friend, or a companion, who will walk alongside them.

Jesus, I thank you for who you are and what you have done. I thank you for the hope we have in you and the reason we can anticipate and long for you to return or call us home. May your Holy Spirit work in our hearts and draw us near to you. I pray that you would do a mighty work in our lives and that after encountering you, we would never be the same. Amen.

MILE 19
ENDURANCE

"The long run is what puts the tiger in the cat."
—Bill Squires

"We are what we repeatedly do. Excellence, then, is not an act but a habit."
—Aristotle

"Moses returned to the Lord and said, 'O Lord, why have you brought trouble upon this people? Is this why you sent me? Ever since I went to Pharaoh to speak in your name, he has brought trouble upon this people, and you have not rescued your people at all.'"
—Exodus 5:22

"By faith Moses, when he had grown up, refused to be known as the son of Pharaoh's daughter. He chose to be mistreated along with the people of God rather than to enjoy the pleasures of sin for a short time. He regarded disgrace for the sake of Christ as of greater value than the treasures of Egypt, because he was looking ahead to his reward. By faith, he left Egypt, not fearing the king's anger, he endured because he saw him who is invisible."
—Hebrews 12:24-27

RUNNING THROUGH LIFE

THROUGHOUT THE MANY miles of training there may be moments where the training runs become monotonous and repetitive. Sometimes different trails need to be run, different running partners need to be established. Perhaps a new band will provide you with the upbeat, adrenaline-pumping music you need. Or maybe not listening to any music at all will help break the steady beat of monotony. With this in mind, we are going to slightly veer from the pattern we have followed in the first eighteen chapters. Rather than view Mile 19 as one long 1600-meter stretch, we are going to split the mile, and the chapter, into four 400-meter segments. By the end of this chapter, the four splits will have added up to one complete mile.

0 meters to 400 meters

We left Chapter Eighteen looking forward. Anticipating the finish line. Earnestly longing for heaven. Yet we are not yet there. As you begin the first 400 meters of Mile 19, I hope there is still a bounce in your step, a smile on your face, and a fire within you that is propelling you toward the finish line. What continues to drive you forward? The likely answer: endurance. Despite fatigue, stress, or other adverse conditions, you have exhibited endurance and are still running.

While you are out running your race, keep your head up and pay attention to those who have gone before you, those who have previously run marathons, and those who are running alongside you. They may have a few things to teach you about endurance. Similarly, those who have gone before us in the race of life are also capable of teaching us a thing or two about endurance.

Moses' race of endurance started shortly after being born. Due to desires of the ruling elite, any newborn male was to be put to death. Rather than adhere to the wishes of the pagan leaders, his mother put him in a basket and placed him in God's hands.

Found in a basket, he was taken in by a princess and therefore grew up in a world of luxury. The walls surrounding him were lush with the best the country had to offer. The education he received was second to none. Daily he learned from the best and brightest. Anything he desired could be given to him with the snap of a finger. Nothing was out of his reach.

In the eyes of many, he lived the good life. But despite the fact that he was living in the Egyptian palace, rubbing shoulders with the rich and glamorous, Moses was called to endure. You see, Moses' heart was striving to glorify God, but he was living in a culture that was glorifying man. Moses had to decide daily between choosing between what would please God and man's sinful desires. His culture taught him to worry about his own needs; his faith taught him to consider others higher than himself. His obedience to God taught him to help the needs of those around him; his palace lifestyle taught him to worry about three things: me, myself, and I. I am certain there were moments when he wanted to give in. Days where he wanted to take the easy route instead of the bumpy course. Yet the way in which he overcame them was through his endurance. He had the strength to continue despite hardships, fatigue, and adverse conditions.

400 meters to 800 meters

Throughout your training you will build up the strength, stamina, and endurance needed to complete a marathon. At times you will be tempted to make excuses: "Well, I ran yesterday's seven at a faster pace than what I wanted, so technically I can afford to lower today's mileage." Or "It has been a long day at work and my mind is fried, I can only do three miles today." While excuses may reap momentary benefits, in the long run (yes, pun intended) they will hurt you.

Throughout your training seek the hills, push yourself when you are tired, and eliminate the little voice inside telling you that skimping on a few miles is a good idea. Focus on building strength, stamina, and endurance. By choosing to do so during your training, you will have the energy to reach your goals on race day. Through the adverse conditions you will have the ability to look around you and enjoy the race.

The word "endurance" is translated from the Greek word *hupomeno*. Literally, *hupo* means "under" and *meno* means "to remain." When you put the two together you get "to remain under." To endure means to continue on, despite being under stress, fatigue, and adverse conditions. Within the world of running, stress, fatigue, and adversity are things that can be anticipated. They can also be prepared for. Your training is an opportunity for you to grow stronger and to allow you to prepare to endure the toll a marathon will put on your body.

While we must train our bodies to be prepared for a marathon, we need to recognize that God will train us to be fit and ready for the work of his kingdom. Perhaps far too often we remember the way in which Moses finished, the way he led the Israelites out of Egypt, across the Red Sea, and through the desert. We remember those times, yet we forget where he started, as a young, brash, and unwilling young man.

Moses' training likely began while he was in Pharaoh's court. In the second chapter of Exodus we see the Israelites groaning in their slavery and crying out to God. Part of Moses' training was being forced to sit silently and watch his fellow citizens being treated brutally as slaves. Perhaps God placed Moses within the Egyptian palace so he could better understand the system and the way in which the Pharaoh operated.

God wanted to train Moses and make him fit and ready to do the work he was called to do. Moses spent time as a shepherd, where he was given the time and space needed to fully rely on God, an attribute he would later need in order to handle a complaining Israelite nation. He experienced a burning bush that would not burn up, helping him understand God's power, a trait that would be replicated as the Red Sea was parted. Leading the Israelites out of Egypt was a task that required endurance, and he had to be at the mercy of God's training before he was ready (if he ever was).

800 meters to 1200 meters

Unfortunately, throughout training there may be certain times when you are headed in the wrong direction. Unplanned setbacks

ENDURANCE

may occur. As much as we would like to completely eliminate them, injuries are a part of running. Pulled muscles. Shin splints. Blisters. Cramps. Stomach issues. Over the course of training as well as running the actual race, many obstacles can overcome you and put you under stress.

Equally damaging can be those burdens that do not attack your body, but blitz your mind. Frustration can easily play a negative role in your performance. You might be discouraged with your pace or disheartened by the weather. Many will go through a period in training where climbing to the next level seems unattainable. Despite your strongest efforts, you may seem to have plateaued and cannot reach a new level. Possibly your setback is a result of lost energy and desire. What once seemed so relaxing and enjoyable has become annoying and difficult. Possibly running was once a way you relieved your stress, and now it is the reason *for* your stress. Nobody wants to believe there are going to be setbacks, frustrations, and times of difficulty while running, yet it is the nature of the beast. It is in these times we must endure, rely on our stamina, and keep moving forward.

The cure for specific setbacks is as unique as the setback itself. Regardless of the setback you're facing, there is one beneficial thing that can be done: looking back and realizing that all along you have been slowly but steadily making improvement. Remember that first ten-mile run? Remember how difficult it was, how tired you were, how badly you wanted to quit? One more mile to go and you will be at twenty, double the distance you were struggling with a month or two ago.

Those sprints that not only took your breath away but also stole your joy and motivation? Now you are smiling through them as they serve as a warm up for your actual workout. Whatever the hurdle, at one point you were not strong enough. Now you are. It did not happen overnight, but it came from your training and your continual effort to move forward. It came from enduring.

Slowly, and often without realizing it, you gain strength and make progress. Moses went through a lot of training and was not fully aware of all that God was doing for the majority of his regimen.

Moses was not ready to lead the people out of Egypt immediately; God had to train him. Moses wanted to do things through his own power. God wanted to do things through his power. Moses, tired, frustrated, and unable to accomplish the task through his own power, cried out to God:

> O Lord, why have you brought trouble upon this people? Is this why you sent me? Ever since I went to Pharaoh to speak in your name, he has brought trouble upon this people, and you have not rescued your people at all.[71]

Moses had a slightly different tone here compared to what we generally focus on. He was stressed, frustrated, even a bit sarcastic. It's as if he was saying, "God, are you still there? Are you sure you got this whole exodus thing correct? You do know we are supposed to be leaving this country, right? You chose me. You told me I was going to help these people. You do realize that these people are being treated brutally, and I'm not the most popular man around the Israelite camp right now, right? I thought I was going to ride into town and be the hero. I was going to show Pharaoh who the real man is. I was ready to have a pyramid erected in my honor, a nice retirement package overlooking the sandy dunes, and work on my golf game at Nile Country Club." Clearly, Moses faced some obstacles.

Yet the most difficult obstacles Moses was facing were not the circumstances surrounding him. They were from the inside, from within his character. Notice how God responds to Moses' whine: "Now you will see what *I* will do to Pharaoh. Because of *my* mighty hand he will let them go; because of *my* mighty hand he will drive them out of his country."[72] Three times God reiterated to Moses, "It is me, not you." Like you, Moses was going through training.

1200 meters to 1600 meters

We left Moses in the fifth chapter of Exodus as he was going through his initial training. Skipping ahead to chapter fourteen

ENDURANCE

we can catch a glimpse of Moses in his "a-ha!" moment, the time where he gets it. Exodus 14:13 reads:

> Moses answered the people, "Do not be afraid. Stand firm and you will see the deliverance the Lord will bring you today. The Egyptians you see today you will never see again. The Lord will fight for you; you need only to be still."

Moses recognized that deliverance would occur because of nothing he or any of the Israelites did. This is a drastically different attitude from the Moses in chapter five. The reason for the difference? His training. The training Moses went through changed his character. The result? Moses triumphed with the exodus of his people.

Your triumph is that you are finished with Mile 19. You only have seven miles left. You have finished over two-thirds of the race. These final 400 meters will bring you even closer to the finish line.

As you move forward, recognize that there will be more to endure. There will be more coming your way. Moses may have led the Israelites out of Egypt, yet following this triumph, they wandered through the desert for forty years. I believe Moses gained strength and courage by looking back at his training. He looked back and remembered the feeling he'd had when he woke up to find frogs hopping all over Egypt. Whenever he cut his foot and saw blood spill, he remembered the way God turned the Nile into blood.

Remember what God has done in your life. Look back at the way he has shown himself faithful, knowing he will do so again. Look back at the strength you gained through your training, recognizing it was worth it and it has enabled you to be where you are today. Look back and allow it to propel you forward.

Father, thank you for Moses and for the many lessons we can learn from him. He was a man just like us. He needed your strength just as we do. Father, help us to endure as Moses did. Help us to move through our training, realizing that you are molding us and shaping us. Thank you for the ways in which you are working, even when we cannot see. Those ways you work and we cannot help but smile and say "a-ha!" Even when we don't have those moments, help us to trust you and rely on your strength. Thank you, Father. Amen.

MILE 20
TENACITY

"It's not the size of the dog in the fight,
it's the size of the fight in the dog."
—Mark Twain

"Never, never, never quit."
—Winston Churchilll

"As Jesus was on his way, the crowds almost crushed him. And a woman was there who had been subject to bleeding for twelve years, but none could heal her. She came up behind him and touched the
edge of his cloak …"
—Mark 8:42b-44a

"Here is a boy with five small barley loaves and two small fish, but how far will they go among so many?"
—John 6:9

HER NAME IS never mentioned. There is very little we ever hear about her. In fact, her story is told in six simple verses.[73] All we know of her life is told in fewer than 120 words, and most of those words aren't even used to describe her or her life. Others overlooked her. Some never even noticed her. Many refused to pay attention to her.

Do you ever wonder about the full stories behind the nameless people of the Bible? In the big picture, many overlook them and label them insignificant. Not worth remembering. Minor. Outcast. Insignificant. Nameless. How many of us feel the same way?

Even though their names were never mentioned, these people have lessons they can teach us, especially the woman who touched Jesus' cloak. As you take a closer look at her story, there is one word that could be used to fully describe her: tenacity. Imagine that. In a book filled with remarkable stories and phenomenal men and women of character, it is a nameless woman who can teach us about such a vital trait. Her story may be brief, but her lesson is monumental. If we apply her wisdom and her examples to our lives, we will be better people, and we will have greater success in our marathon running.

Even prior to unveiling the jewels of this woman's story, I hope you are encouraged. If you feel small, overlooked, insignificant, or nameless, realize that you can have an incredible impact. Regardless of the length of your personal résumé, you serve the living, omniscient, omnipotent creator of the universe. He desires to work in and through you. You can be his hands and feet.

Although few words are used to describe this woman, it becomes clear that she was full of tenacity. She possessed a spirit that was unwilling to give up. She was tough. She was persistent. In looking at her life, we see at least three reasons why she could have decided against showing up and pursuing Jesus. First, there were many people in the area. In Luke's account he writes that the crowds almost crushed him (Jesus).[74] She was one of hundreds, probably thousands. Second, she was physically sick and weak. At this point in her life she had been bleeding for twelve consecutive years. It wasn't the ideal condition to be in while trying to fight through a

TENACITY

massive crowd. Third, she was a woman. I say that with no ill intent to females. Historically and within the cultural context, women were looked down upon. Within her culture, being a woman was a disadvantage. One of thousands. Physically weak. Socially inferior. The average person may have stayed home. Yet this woman was far from average. She was tenacious.

My initial focus was on this woman and her ability to overcome these obstacles, ultimately reaching Jesus. I began to wonder what I would have done in her position. She overcame obstacles that most would use as excuses. Would anyone blame her for not fighting through a massive crowd? After all, she suffered from intense bleeding. Wouldn't the elbows and shoves of a large multitude only add to her physical pain? There are plenty of excuses as to why she shouldn't have met Jesus. But then it hit me. The excuses were not excuses. They were lies. They were lies from those who attempt to keep people from reaching Jesus. However, the lies were no match for the tenacity within her as she strove to touch Jesus. Regardless of time or place, there are many lies that our enemies will try to make us believe.

Lie number one: Jesus has more important things to handle than you.

This woman was one in a sea of people. The crowd was so large that they almost crushed Jesus. Many within the crowd needed healing, needed the touch of a Savior. In fact, the main plot of this portion of scripture is about a rich and powerful man whose daughter is deathly ill. Can you hear the lies as they are whispered into her ear? "You are just one person among all these people. Why do you think Jesus would have time for you? Who or what makes you think you are above the others? Look at all the people around you, certainly they are much more important."

If the words of doubt pouring from Satan's mouth were not enough, those in the crowd also joined the chorus. Each step brought her closer to Jesus. Yet each step also exposed her to a new set of judging eyes. I do not know the heart of those in the crowd; the text does not say. His disciples were there with him, so there were clearly those who were full of Christ's love, mercy, and compassion. Yet even his disciples were sinners, prone to selfishness, uncontrolled tongues, and pride. In order for this woman to reach Jesus she had to fight through what others thought of her.

Lie number two: You have too much baggage to be of use to God's kingdom.

Another obstacle she had to overcome was her physical condition. I, in my weakness, look at her physical condition and come to the conclusion that I would not blame her for using her physical condition as a reason to give up. Put her condition into perspective. If you roll an ankle you may be sidelined for a few weeks, maybe a month. A pulled muscle? With proper treatment and therapy you could recover and be back to normal within a few months. With today's advanced technology and medicine, a broken leg, even a torn ACL, could sideline you for only twelve to eighteen months. I am not trying to belittle those injuries. Yet when compared to this woman who had been bleeding for twelve years, they seem like minor scrapes. Do not be too quick to disregard the amount of time she was suffering.

Think back to where you were twelve years ago. Twelve years ago you may have had a child going through the "terrible two's." Now that child is in high school. Think back to when you were in kindergarten. If you fast forward twelve years from that point, you would be walking across the stage receiving a high school diploma. A lot changes in twelve years. However, this woman's condition had not improved. She had likely visited every doctor in the area. She probably spent every penny she had on medicine, hoping that something would cure her. For twelve years she visited doctors. For twelve years she spent her financial resources. For twelve years she was in physical pain and never healed.

Instead of preventing her from getting to Jesus, this woman's physical condition is what drove her to Jesus. I am certain that Satan did not want her to reach Jesus. I imagine his lies were along the lines of, "What do you believe you have to offer? Look at your pain! Look at your past! Do you really think Jesus wants to embrace someone with a past like yours?"

Lie number three: You're an outcast, nobody could love you, you're not good enough.

The third obstacle that had to be overcome was her social standing as a female and the fact that in the eyes of just about everyone, she was not worth anything. In the opinion of those around her she had no privileges, no rights, and nothing major to offer society. She had been beaten with lies that attacked her faith and her mindset. Now, with eyes looking down at her, she felt insignificant and worthless. Yet the amazing thing is that the eyes of others did not matter to her. She was only seeking the affection of one person, and in his eyes she was worthy of love. In fact, she was worth so much he was willing to leave his eternal throne to take her sins, and the sins of the entire world.

She had to walk through the crowds and listen to the jeers and criticisms they hurled at her. Certainly the many elbows in the stomach hurt, but even more painful were the words aimed at her. I imagine there are a number of people who can readily identify with her.

Have you ever had co-workers judge and mock you because of your faith? When everyone else decides to go to the strip club to celebrate the closing of the deal and you stay back, do cries of mockery flow as readily as their alcohol? Perhaps at one point prior to encountering the love of Jesus you would join your co-workers, but now you no longer choose to be involved in those activities. Do you hear their taunts reminding you of your baggage—the sneering of those who try to make you believe your sinful past is bigger than God's grace?

What about while you are running? Do you face the same things? Some may look at your running history, or lack thereof, and throw seeds of doubt at you, claiming you will never have the strength, determination, or ability to complete a marathon. They minimize your efforts by throwing out numbers of how many people regularly run, and highlight reasons why each and every one of those runners is more talented and more capable. Or how many try and never actually complete a marathon. Lies pile up that captivate your energy and enthusiasm. Excuses appear to be an easier route, rather than the one that leads to the finish line.

Do not give up. Fend off the devil's lies. Follow the lead of this nameless woman. Be tenacious.

The more I think about her, the more encouraged I become. She met Jesus and was forever changed because she decided to tenaciously follow him. She was tough. She was persistent. She was vicious in her pursuit. She refused to give in and quit. She refused to listen to those around her, knowing she was chasing after the way, the truth, and the life. She realized she had baggage, but knew he had the power to take it away.

I imagine her struggling down the road toward the boat Jesus just embarked from. He has only taken a few steps on solid land before the massive crowd encircles him. She screams his name; she desperately desires to get his attention. Those around her push her down, tell her to shut up, or tell her to go home. She fights through the first wave of people only to get pushed over and thrown to the ground. The bleeding gets worse with each person she tries to push past. She gets knocked down, but refuses to stay on the ground. Unwilling to concede defeat, she once again sees Jesus, fervently chasing after him. Now in the thick of the crowd, the jeers increase in volume and magnitude. She tunes them out in an attempt to better hear his voice. As he stops to pick up a little child, the crowd suddenly stops, causing people to bump into each other. Once again she is thrown to the ground and trampled over. Down on the ground she sees hundreds of legs. Knowing this is her opportunity, she crawls towards him. Now her knees get scraped up, and they too start bleeding. But then! Then she sees the feet of the one they call Jesus. She reaches out, grabs his cloak, and is instantly healed. This woman had such a tenacious pursuit of Jesus.

As you run Mile 20, I hope you have a tenacious spirit, a spirit that refuses to listen to the lies of those around you regarding your

TENACITY

running ability, and a sharp mind that overcomes the physical pain you have been in or are about to experience. Don't quit. You are almost there. Be tenacious and keep moving toward the finish line.

More important than running, I hope that your walk with Jesus parallels that of this unnamed woman. May your walk be tenacious. Despite the troubles of this world, regardless of the lies you are fed, tenaciously follow Jesus. When obstacles come your way, keep your eyes fixed on him, the author and perfecter of our faith.[75] When the taunts of those around you attempt to break your spirit, listen for his voice and his truth. Be tenacious in your pursuit of Jesus.

Father, thank you for loving us. Thank you for caring about us, and caring for us. Thank you for accepting us despite our baggage, regardless of our past. Thank you for grace and mercy that is bigger than our baggage. Thank you for the example of the nameless. May the story of this woman be an encouragement to all who read it. May they admire her tenacity and emulate it. May we be a people who tenaciously follow you. Amen.

MILE 21
ENCOURAGEMENT

"Promise me you'll always remember: You're braver than
you believe, and stronger than you seem,
and smarter than you think."
(Christopher Robin to Pooh)
—Alan Alexander Milne

"Correction does much, but encouragement does more."
—Johann Wolfgang von Goethe

"The angel said to the woman, 'Do not be afraid …'"
—Matthew 28:5

"We always thank God, the Father of our Lord Jesus
Christ, when we pray for you, because we have heard of
your faith in Christ Jesus and of the love you
have for all the saints …"
—Colossians 1:3-4

*I*T WAS RATHER simple. My guess is that nobody else on the field saw it. Most likely, in the few seconds immediately following the action, the only other person involved completely forgot about it. Yet to me, it was a gesture and a moment that signaled greater things than intended. It was something I had been longing for and desperately needing. It was a moment I view as an emotional and cultural turning point. The action that provided waves of encouragement was a simple high-five followed by, *"Gut spiel, Tommy! Klasse."*

I was on the soccer field playing with a German team I had recently joined. There are two or three guys who speak a minimal amount of English, and I speak even less German. Communicating has proven to be very difficult and extremely frustrating. After a few weeks, I slowly started to figure out how to say certain things while playing on the field. I found myself wanting to speak my natural language of communication, English. However, I knew I had to decide what to say in English, translate and figure out how to say it in German, and then actually say it. By the time my brain went through those gymnastics, the speed of the game rendered my comments useless and ill-timed.

For weeks I would attend training and matches unable to communicate. Team meetings would follow a training session and the coach would draw diagrams on the chalkboard, talking through game strategy. For forty-five minutes I would sit and listen to sounds without understanding the words. Though my level of communication has slowly increased, it is still terrible.

My confidence does not find its roots in what others think of me. My vision of myself as a soccer player is not influenced by what others say. However, I have recently realized how important it can be for everyone to receive a pat on the back and an "atta boy!" or "atta girl!" every now and then. I was not dependent on my teammates' approval, yet the lack of encouragement was disappointing.

Something as simple as a high-five can do wonders. For fourteen weeks I had been training with the team, and for fourteen weeks I had not received one word of encouragement. I would come in and out of training having worked hard, pushed myself, played well,

ENCOURAGEMENT

and heard nothing from my coaches or teammates. In the matches, I would contribute to the team—I even scored a goal—and still go without receiving any positive feedback … until that practice. I had stolen the ball from the other team, dribbled past one defender, and slid a pass through to a teammate who took a shot and scored. As my teammate Hille ran back to his position, he gave me a high-five and said, *"Gut spiel, Tommy! Klasse!"* A few encouraging words. A simple act. Two things everyone else probably failed to recognize. Two things Hille may have forgotten about as soon as play resumed. Two things that spurred my confidence, gave me encouragement, and provided me with a much-needed boost.

Mile 21. You are in the twenties. The finish line is getting increasingly close. Thoughts of "just a few more" start to infiltrate your mind. You repeat your running mantras with more fervor and frequency. You have been persistent, tenacious, and dedicated. You are nearing the end but are not quite there. The journey may take you up a few more hills. Your body is craving to be shut down; muscles may be cramping. The smile you once had is fading. The thrill of the first few miles is nothing but a distant memory. You, my friend, are in need of some encouragement.

Encouragement will look and sound different to different people. As a coach of a high school girls' soccer team, I try to understand the uniqueness of each player. One player responds positively as I raise my voice and give seemingly stern instruction. Another hears the same tone and shrivels up, fearing rejection or complete disapproval. Some need a balance of the things they are doing poorly, complemented by the things they are doing well. Regardless of what method is used to encourage, encouragement's effects cannot be argued. Encouragement provides you with energy, enthusiasm, desire, and passion. Encouragement reminds you of your goal, your destination, and your purpose. Encouragement inspires. It helps. It carries. It fills you with courage.

Encouragement fills you with courage. Recognizing this, take a journey back to the very first chapter where we witnessed two men who had extreme courage, and as a result radically influenced the vantage point of those who witnessed them. Joshua and Caleb showed us that courage provides us with the ability to speak truth when others are afraid to. Esther highlighted the ability to stand up for what she knew was right. Peter and John rubbed shoulders with Jesus and their lives were forever changed.

Similar to these giants of the biblical faith, you, too, are a character of courage within your own realm of influence, but also in your willingness to cross the starting line and begin the steps of a marathon. As you run through the twenty-first mile, may I remind you of the courage that is within you? The courage that was able to overpower the voices of doubt that mocked you as you took the very first step of a 26.2 mile journey? As you started your race you had a mind and spirit of courage—and you still do! Even after twenty miles, that mind and heart in possession of the ability to face adversity, danger, and challenge still belongs to you. Courage is not simply the fortitude to face the situation, but the resolve to do so without fear, and with a confident, unabashed spirit.

As you run your race, it is my hope that you do not rely on others for encouragement, but that you also do not shy away from encouragement when it comes your way. The encouragement you need will come from a variety of people. Never allow yourself to belittle or ignore those at the aid stations providing you with nourishment for the body—water and food—but equally as important nourishment for the mind and soul—encouragement. Humbly allow yourself to realize they are there for you. Their job is to equip and enable you to run the best race you can. As they stand there to provide for you, allow them to fill you up. Take what they have to offer, both water and words, and allow it to replenish you. As they hand you water, thank them. As they smile at you, smile back. As they clap for you, acknowledge them. They are there to encourage you and to help you move forward.

In addition to the race volunteers, encouragement can come from the random spectators who are observing and enjoying the race. In my experience it has been these individuals who have provided a great amount of encouragement. More specifically, it is the young spectators, the children who are cheering even though they are unable to explain the difference between a 100-meter

ENCOURAGEMENT

sprint and a marathon. They are not aware of the monumental task being undertaken. They are unfamiliar with the training you went through, or the pain you are currently going through. But there they are. Cheering. Clapping. Screaming. Encouraging. Not because they understand, but rather because they are completely oblivious. Whether it takes ten months or ten years for them to fully realize the magnitude of what they are watching, in that moment they are cheering because you are you, for no other reason other than you have a bib and a number, and are running.

Equally as encouraging are those who know all too well what you are going through—the fellow runners who feel your pain, sense your struggle, and share your path. They can encourage because they have been there. They can offer words to uplift you since they are on the same journey. Perhaps it is those in your running group who have logged every training mile with you and are now still by your side through the twenty-first mile. However, it might be those you have never met prior to race day. They are running with you, stride by stride beside you. Their words bring truth and have power because they understand. They encourage you because they are there with you, going through the battle and fighting right alongside you.

In connection with a marathon, there are generally three different timeframes in which we can receive encouragement—before, during, and after the race. In thinking through each of these timeframes, I thought of a specific individual who had provided me encouragement during that period.

Prior to my marathons, it was always my dad who provided me with the words of encouragement I needed. My dad is a huge influence on my life and one of the people who means the most to me. He has continually been a blessing and a source of encouragement, strength, and wisdom. There were many times when my dad would ask questions about my training, my mileage, or how I was feeling. Additionally, as he saw fit he would offer advice and words of wisdom. He was an avid runner and has a few marathons under his belt, so his opinion is one that not only had weight because he was my dad, but because he had experience as well. To this day I have yet to run a marathon faster than him, but that is one thing I hope to change in the near future! As I look back at the races I have run, it was definitely my dad who was there providing me with the encouragement I needed prior to the race.

During the race is another vital time in which you need encouragement. Thankfully I feel blessed because there are a number of different people I could highlight who have been there for me during the race. One instance continually comes to mind. The third marathon I ran was in Freiburg, Germany, a city about forty-five minutes away from where I live. Given the proximity, there were a few different groups who came out to support me, one of whom was one of my closest friends in Germany, Brandon. He and his wife, Lizzy, have been great friends of mine throughout my entire time in Germany, and it has been a blessing to walk side by side with them in our ministry here. On this particular day they both came out to support me and cheer me on. Somewhere around the seventh mile I spotted them. This in itself was ideal timing, as the seventh mile was a time when I was struggling and starting to feel the initial toll of the race. The sun was beating down, draining my energy and hydration. The course had been challenging, and at that point I was in need of some encouragement. As I came through the seventh mile I saw my "posse" on the sideline cheering me on. Brandon was not content on the sidewalk, so he hopped onto the road (which I do not encourage anyone to do) and he jogged with me for a couple hundred meters. During those steps I talked the entire time. I talked about how I was struggling, how I was feeling, what I was wishing for, what my race plans were, etc. He simply jogged and listened. We continued to jog together for a few more steps, he patted me on the back and off I went. I later found out that as he returned to the rest of the group they asked, "What did Tommy say?" to which Brandon replied, "I don't really know. A bunch of stuff about running and distances and numbers, nothing I really understand at all."

Brandon jogged with me during the race. He filled me with encouragement and excitement. He did not do so through any magical words, because it was I who did all the talking. But he was there with me. He was listening to me, even if he didn't understand exactly what I was talking about. That was encouraging. In addition to all of that, that particular day happened to be Brandon's birthday. To have a friend choose to spend his birthday by coming and watching you run a marathon is something extremely special.

There are times when you will need encouragement when everything is over. That might sound odd—the race is finished. Why is encouragement needed at that point? In the race I mentioned above, I finished fifty-five minutes slower than my goal. I had trained hard. I had been dedicated. I was focused. I had a goal, and I missed it—by a lot. Following the race I was flooded with a variety of emotions, one of which was discouragement. I was discouraged by my performance and the time it took me to complete the race. In the heat of my discouragement, in came Jim. He had been the ring leader of my cheering section that day. He had organized the rides, corralled the people, and scouted out the different markers to be at during the race. After the race he was the first person to find me, and immediately put his arms around me, gave me a hug, and spoke of how proud he was. I didn't feel proud; I was embarrassed. Jim didn't see me as a failure, he saw me as a champion. Jim didn't see what I failed to accomplish, he recognized what I had accomplished. For those initial moments after the race, and for the days and weeks to come, he did nothing but fill me with encouragement.

For the next two months every time I bumped into him he mentioned the race. Every time he was full of excitement and encouragement. "Man, Tommy, wasn't that a great race? Have I told you how well you did?" Comments flowed from his mouth, and you could not help but recognize the sincerity in his voice. "You did such a good job. We were there for you and cheering for you, and you didn't let us down. You were terrific." There were moments when I wanted to forget about the race and act as if it never happened, yet Jim always reminded me of my accomplishment, regardless of whether I made my goal. Upon meeting someone new, Jim would immediately say, "Have you met Tommy? He just ran a marathon. He did fantastic. He is a champion."

After the race I was filled with disgust, embarrassment, and discouragement. A little voice inside of me kept saying, "You were awful. You didn't do well at all today. Ha, you thought you were prepared, guess what ... you weren't!" The voice was gnawing at my confidence; it was running away with my joy in finishing. "You're too weak. You didn't want it bad enough." Those were horrible things to hear, and after a while they started taking root. Any time they tried to fill my mind, Jim came in and spoke words of encouragement. His words were filled with life, truth, excitement, and passion. Soon his words overpowered and replaced that little voice. It was no longer discouraging to think about the race, but encouraging.

Before the race, during the race, and after the race. All are times when encouragement is helpful, beneficial, and needed. The same could be said for our spiritual walk.

It might seem odd to talk about encouragement you can receive prior to your spiritual walk. How can you receive encouragement for something you have yet to start? How can you be prepared for something you are not even fully aware of? In our finite human minds, questions like these can be baffling. However, we do not serve a God with a finite human mind; rather, we serve a God who spoke the universe into existence. We serve a God who always was, always is, and always will be. Therefore, it is not outside of his capability to prepare us for something prior to any humans having any inkling it could happen.

As we view some encouragement, I find no other person more appropriate to look at than Jesus himself. In Matthew 18:20 Jesus declares, "Where two or three come together in my name, there am I with them." What an incredible promise and what an amazing piece of encouragement. When we gather together as believers in Christ, Jesus has promised to be there with us. This goes along with God's promise to Joshua when he said, "I will never leave you nor forsake you."[76] Jesus always was, always is, and always will be. Our race as a Christian has a beginning point. That is not the case with Jesus. With that in mind, prior to Jesus' earthly departure he left

ENCOURAGEMENT

us a promise indicating that he will be with us. That news should fill us with courage.

Another way in which Jesus encourages us is through his prayers. In John 17 we have a written account of Jesus' prayer. Jesus prays for all of the believers. Stop and think about that for a second. Jesus, the only son of God, the perfect Savior, went before the throne of God the Father, on our behalf. Jesus went before the Father to pray for us, to intercede for us. This happened before you or I were born; yet Jesus knew us all by name, and when he prayed for all the believers, he was praying for us.

As I mentioned above, there are also times where we need encouragement during the race. Certain circumstances in life can hinder us, cause our run to become a crawl, slow us down, and cause us to lose focus. At times such as these, when someone comes alongside you and whispers a few words of encouragement in your ear, your spirit is renewed.

Through coaching I have realized some people need a good yell to get them in motion. However, there are others who need a calm, gentle whisper. As I read through the story of Mary at Jesus' tomb, I saw her receive such a whisper. The odd part is it came from an angel who had just caused an earthquake and rolled back a massive stone. Matthew describes the angel's arrival accompanied by an earthquake, an appearance as bright as lightning and clothes as white as snow.[77] Quite an appearance. The guards certainly thought so. They quickly became filled with fear and fell to the ground like dead men.

While there is never any mention of the tone of the angel's voice, most probably assume the voice was a deep, powerful, booming voice. Something that Hollywood would produce. But I see the angel's words coming more as a whisper, and more friendly than some booming, earth-shattering voice. The first words are, "Do not be afraid." The angel had an incredible entrance, rolled back the stone, and then sat on it. With such a powerful entrance, he then seems to be so, dare I say, relaxed. I imagine the angel sitting there, cracking a smile as he sees the guards fall down, and gently, calmly, and lovingly telling Mary to not be afraid.

Mary has every right to be afraid and startled. It is not every day you get visited by an angel, especially one who enters in such a grand fashion. But in the midst of her fear the angel calmly encourages her not to be afraid. I wonder, did the angel descend from his perch on the stone, and come down and stand next to Mary? I like to think his words were calm, gentle, heart-filled words of encouragement. Mary took the words of the angel to heart, and followed the instructions given to her. As she departed she was still afraid, yet the text also says she was filled with joy. What an amazing picture. Someone coming alongside you in the middle of your race, at a time that is unexpected, but much needed. The gentle whisper, to not be afraid. The calming smile, the heart-filling peace. And after the words you are on your way, filled with joy.

There will be times after your race when you may be in need of encouragement. While the ultimate finish line will not be crossed until we depart from this earth, there are different chapters that we will finish between now and then. I see this played out through Paul's writing to the church at Colosse. At the outset of his letter, Paul writes to this body of believers and encourages them by giving a report of their faith and the fruit of their labor. These believers are receiving a note that is in essence saying, "You guys are doing a great job. We are continually hearing about your love for each other and the way in which you are spreading the Gospel of Jesus Christ." Paul had interaction with these believers and following that interaction he felt the necessity to go back and encourage them in their faith. There seems to be little doubt that those receiving this letter would be filled with courage as they hear how their brother in Christ had witnessed their faith and had seen the fruit of their faith grow to life. Since Paul had witnessed these things, he desired to encourage them and in so doing he also encourages us to follow his pattern.

If we were to walk away from this chapter and simply gather insight into how others can encourage us, we would miss the point. I hope you also recognize that, although it is important to receive encouragement, it is far greater to be the one who is supplying others with encouragement.

ENCOURAGEMENT

I challenge you to pray a very simple, yet profound prayer. It is perhaps the most common prayer I offer to God. Often while I am running, I will pray to God and simply say, "Lord, please show me those in my sphere of influence who are in need of encouragement." After praying those words I visualize those near me. It is as if my mind starts a slideshow, and I scan through different photos of those around me. I scroll until I feel the Lord tug on my heart and nudge me to do what I can to encourage that person or persons. It is amazing to see the way in which God answers this prayer. As you finish Mile 21 of your race, I encourage you to pray about those within your sphere of influence who could use encouragement.

There have been numerous people throughout my life who have encouraged me, and helped shape me into the man I am. For the ways they have blessed me and encouraged me, I am forever grateful.

One night while trying to fall asleep I was reviewing the day I had just gone through—the highs, and the lows, and the moments of frustration. As I was thinking about the day, I was struck by whom I had spent time with. It was a bit weird looking back because I knew that while the day was going on there was no question or hesitation on my part. I hung out with certain students and it felt natural. It felt like an easy decision. As I lay trying to fall asleep, I began chuckling to myself and whispered, "Mom, I blame you." Now I really do not blame her in a negative way, but I realized she was extremely influential in raising me in such a way that my eyes are continually open to those students who need a friend, who need someone to come alongside them, who do not easily fit in, or who may seem to get lost in the crowd. I lay there blaming my mom, when in all reality, I was realizing how blessed I was to have been raised and encouraged to act in such a way. Thankful for this realization, I flipped over, hoping a new position would bring with it some needed rest.

Still unable to fall asleep, I asked myself two questions: "Why am I the way I am?" and "Why do I do what I do?" In pondering these questions, I came up with some answers I feel compelled to share.

Because of my mom, I try to see the best in people. I have a heart that wants to love the unlovable. I strive to make others feel as though they are a part of a group, and that they belong, regardless of what their peers may think or say.

I refuse to give in. I refuse to give up. I choose to persevere and keep going. I do this because my sister, Whitney, has modeled for me what it is to persevere. She has demonstrated an attitude that is unwilling to settle for what others may deem impossible, and makes it possible. When others say, "You can't," she says, "I can, and I will."

I write notes in hope of being a blessing to others. Receiving a personal handwritten note has the power to change an attitude, and take you from a point of frustration to a point of happiness. I know this because after an incredible journey from Maine to Florida I received a note from my friend Croce as we sat in the Jacksonville airport. That note has given me more strength than I can write about, as it has stayed in my wallet since the day I first read it.

I persist in wanting to truly know how people are doing, growing unsatisfied with surface-level answers that do not honestly answer the question, "How are you doing?" Why do I do this? Jack. For an entire soccer season he refused my initial response to "How are you feeling?" until I took off the mask I was hiding behind. He persisted with me—and now, I do the same with others.

I grow facial hair now because for four straight years I received ridicule from Ross because I couldn't. Of course, it didn't help he could daily produce a furry rug of hair—on his face, chest, and back.

I seek adventure, and feel the strength to stand up for what I believe, knowing that I have a brother, Philip, who will always have my back regardless of where I go or what I do.

I no longer dread saying goodbye as I once did, after seeing my friendship with Free be maintained and even strengthened, despite great distances and even greater time between being in the presence of one another.

I have chosen to make cinnamon rolls for a dorm, after waking up on many Saturday mornings after a sleepover with the scent of bubble bread spreading throughout the house. With each bite my

ENCOURAGEMENT

taste buds were awakened, causing them to dance and rejoice over the cinnamon goodness. Again, I blame my mom for this.

I have come to enjoy super-deep conversations as a result of rubbing shoulders with AJ. At the same time, coming to an understanding that it is OK to go deep, especially when you have huge muscles.

I laugh and use my humor to enrich and liven situations after watching my dad use humor when skies were gray and smiles were hard to come by. Wisdom, strength, and laughter infiltrate my actions, resulting from being his son.

When I play soccer I think back to playing with Bear and the white hot rage, knowing that it is simply the only way to play.

I enjoy studying Scripture after having conversations with Manny and seeing the direct and powerful impact it has had on his daily life and everyone with whom he interacts.

I enjoy meeting new people after having a random freshman roommate who turned into a lifelong friend. The start of a friendship can prove to be extremely entertaining and full of adventure if your friend suddenly has a violent reaction to poison ivy within the first month of living together.

As I write, the season of autumn is upon us and nothing signals autumn to me more than a soft snickerdoodle washed down by a hot glass of apple cider. This combination will always bring a smile as I remember the miles my grandparents traveled every autumn in order to watch me play soccer. Along with great conversation and fellowship they brought a jug of apple cider and a coffee tin full of snickerdoodles. I plan on making these treats for some students with the hope they will be filled with love and joy in the same way my grandparents filled me.

As I try to sleep I get a better understanding of why I do what I do, and why I am the way I am. So many of the things I do are a direct result of what others have done in my life. The ways in which Christ has shaped and changed them have changed me. When Christ pours out of your life, he pours into my life. For the things mentioned, both serious and entertaining, I have been encouraged, and I thank those responsible.

Father, thank you for all those who supply us with encouragement. Please give us the eyes to see those around us who are in need of some encouragement. Then give us the strength, energy, obedience, courage, wisdom, and opportunity to deliver that encouragement. Amen.

MILE 22
EXHAUSTION

"The vision of a champion is bent over, drenched in sweat, at the point of exhaustion, when nobody else is looking."
—Mia Hamm

"I firmly believe that any man's finest hour, his greatest fulfillment to all he holds dear, is the moment when he has worked his heart out in a good cause and lies exhausted, but victorious, on the field of battle."
—Vince Lombardi

"Come to me all you who are weary and heavy burdened and I will give you rest."
—Matthew 11:28

DRAINED. WORN OUT. Fatigued. How often have those words accurately described how you were feeling? They might ring true as you push through Mile 22. It is not only during the race itself that these words hold true. It is common to use these words when describing the days and months of training for a marathon. Additionally, these words can describe the exhaustion our hearts so often feel. Times of exhaustion are inevitable, both in running and in life. There can be no denying the reality of exhaustion, yet the questions remain—what do we do and where do we turn when we are exhausted?

Throughout the training period it is not uncommon to grow increasingly tired. This weariness may be physical in nature as the weeks of high mileage take a toll on your body. It may be that the monotony of running day after day has led to dullness and lack of passion. Perhaps the dedication and discipline required of you are wearing you down. Regardless of the specifics behind the exhaustion, it must be dealt with.

For those who are struggling with the physical toll that can occur from all the training miles, realize you are not alone. Take a deep breath, knowing that most people hit a wall during their training. As you get further along in your training regimen, I offer you four simple words of advice: listen to your body. There will be days when you need to take an extra day off. As you take that day off, you do not need to feel guilty about it. Taking a day off to recover, rest, relax, and think about things other than running can be a very positive and beneficial activity.

After weeks of training you should start to understand your body and what it is communicating to you. When your body is begging you for a slower run, a shorter run, or no run at all, do not be afraid to listen to it. After you have built a solid base of miles, you can afford to take a day off. Your speed will not drastically decrease if you take one day off. In fact, if you listen to your body and take an occasional day off, your time might actually improve. In case you need a reminder, you are not running a sprint; you are running a marathon. The race itself will take multiple hours, and the training will take multiple months.

EXHAUSTION

You might find yourself becoming mentally exhausted from the monotony of running day in and day out, running the same trail, the same hills, or the same thing over and over. In many ways running your favorite trail can be beneficial. You can use landmarks to help time yourself. However, sometimes when you know every inch of the trail ahead of you, your excitement, passion, and overall running outlook can dwindle. For example, you realize the bridge overlooking the park leads to a dreadful incline that you really don't want to run. The terrain is always the same and so there is nothing new or out of the ordinary to challenge you. Running the same routes can lead you to a point where your attitude toward running becomes listless or somewhat apathetic.

Change. Seek out a new path. Rather than running alone, find a friend to run with. Tired of running the same hills? Find some flat terrain to give your legs a bit of a break. Be creative. Keep your mind and spirit energetic by continually changing things. Doing so will help prevent you from exhausting your energy and motivation to run.

Far too often it seems as though being tired and exhausted is directly synonymous with weakness. It is as if the words carry a massive negative connotation. However, going through periods of exhaustion throughout your training is not reason for concern, discouragement, or worry. Everyone gets tired. In the same sense, it is important to know that times of exhaustion will occur in our spiritual lives as well. When those inevitable times of spiritual fatigue hit, do not become discouraged.

Exhaustion is a disease in our society that often does not go unnoticed but does go untreated. The world in which we live is tired. Many different reasons can be given as to why people are tired—jobs, kids, school, etc. The number of tasks overshadows the number of hours.

When an individual reaches the point of exhaustion, feelings of desperation creep in. At this point people will seek to do whatever they can to rid themselves of their fatigue. Many will find relief, but most of the time it is only temporary. When one avenue no longer provides the relief and shelter we are searching for, it is time to move to the next source of temporary liberation. Many will hopelessly and aimlessly move from one fleeting relief to the next. However, there is one source, one place, to which individuals can turn to receive permanent deliverance from a tired and weary world. This escape is found in Matthew 11:28, where Jesus exclaims, "Come to me."

This passage and the way our society treats this passage reminds me of the old nursery rhyme, "Humpty Dumpty." The rhyme goes:

> Humpty Dumpty sat on a wall,
> Humpty Dumpty had a great fall.
> All the king's horses and all the king's men
> Couldn't put Humpty together again.

If one has the chance to read this story from a picture book it is not uncommon to see Humpty illustrated as an egg. Why an egg? Eggs are easily broken, and when an egg is broken, the shattered shell is nearly impossible to piece back together. Humans are just like the egg, Humpty Dumpty. Our society crushes us, leaving us mentally, physically, emotionally, and spiritually drained. We, just like Humpty, have fallen from the wall. Life is not easy, and it often brings periods of disappointment. Not all seasons of exhaustion will be the same for every person, but they will come. The weariness of life will bring a great gust of wind that will blow us off the wall and leave us on the ground shattered, destroyed, and desperately searching for someone or something to rescue us.

For a while it seems as though Humpty has some relief. Imagine his excitement and the thoughts that crossed his mind as he heard "all the king's horses and all the king's men" were on their way to help him. Perhaps he was honored that the king himself would send all of his men and horses. Maybe he was embarrassed when word got out how scrambled he had become. Regardless, Humpty likely believed that he would be relieved from his desperate situation. No longer would the crushing impact of the fall leave him broken and helpless. Humpty probably anticipated being put back together in order to resume the life he was accustomed to living. A few quick fixes from the king's horses and men, and Humpty would be back on the wall just as if he had never fallen!

EXHAUSTION

Can you relate to Humpty Dumpty, distressed and shattered? In the darkness of desperation there seems to be a light and a solution to the problem. Perhaps the winds of loneliness knocked you off the wall and in order to feel complete and whole you turn to pornography. Perhaps you are tired and worn out from your job's stresses and demands, so upon coming home you neglect your family and plop on the sofa to watch TV, in the hope of drowning out any and all distractions and worries. Humpty Dumpty was ecstatic upon hearing of the arrival of all the king's men and all the king's horses. In the same way, many eager await the arrival of a Friday night spent drinking away the long work week. Humpty Dumpty is not simply an old nursery rhyme; it is the story of many people's lives. Just as Humpty dreamed of what could be fixed by the king's entourage, we, too, place far too much hope in things of this world to cure our exhaustion.

Humpty received momentary relief at the sight of the messengers from the king, but to no avail. "All the king's horses and men could not put Humpty together again." Alcohol, drugs, TV, sex, material possessions—these are the avenues we pursue in the hope of relief. Many are lonely and searching for companionship, believing this void can be filled through having many promiscuous sex partners. Yet every time a partner leaves the bed, the bedroom feels emptier than it was before. Perhaps there will be a few moments, days, or even years of relief and belief that the pain has been eliminated. However, the alcohol, drugs, and TV will not be more than temporary reliefs to our desperate situations.

This is where the story of Humpty Dumpty ends. Humpty is not put back together again. When you think about it, it truly is a sad story. It does not finish like a normal childhood rhyme or story where everyone lives "happily ever after." In this story we leave Humpty Dumpty a broken, destroyed, incomplete mess. Perhaps things would have differed greatly if Humpty had turned to the king rather than settling for the king's men. What if Humpty would not have been satisfied with the arrival of the king's horses and men, but demanded the king himself come? Imagine if we would put an end to our settling for TV, drugs, and sex and went to our King in heaven for fulfillment? When life leaves us shattered, broken, and incomplete, it is then that Jesus states, "Come to me all you who are weary and heavy laden and I will give you rest."[78]

Think about the claim that is made in those words. Jesus is stating that he can give us rest. Jesus is implying that we need not go searching for rest from anything else—all we need and all we could ever want is in him. Not only does Jesus want to give us rest, he invites all to "take my yoke upon you, and learn from me."[79] Jesus invites us to walk side-by-side with him, and he implores us to allow him to carry what we cannot carry on our own. Jesus asks us to allow him to be the one to put us back together again.

God not only invites us to join him, but also encourages us to learn from him. God will reveal to us ways to prevent ourselves from falling off the wall again. Jesus will instruct us and guide us away from certain difficulties. Jesus will teach us how to break free from the addictions and struggles that have left us broken, shattered, and exhausted. Above all, Jesus will teach us how to trust him.

Matthew 11:28 is commonly quoted and referenced, and rightfully so as it is a beautiful promise from Jesus. However, after hearing it for many years it may be far too easy to allow the verses and the promise to become something we recite without any meaning. We may read the passage on a poster in passing and refuse to pause and reflect on the words. Are these mere words on a bookmark that give cause for a random smile every now and then? Or do these words hold enough power to be life changing?

Picture the scene. Jesus was speaking to a large crowd in the afternoon. They are just off the sea, so there is a gentle sea breeze that brings refreshment to a very warm summer day. There is a great feeling of anticipation in the crowd as they are about to hear a man named Jesus speak. The crowd has heard of this man for many months now but many have not had the opportunity to see him or hear him speak. They heard rumors about his healing powers and his audacious claims. There are some who want to stone him and catch him in a lie for all the questionable statements he has made. Others have given up their careers to follow him and travel with him. Many in the crowd wonder which side of the fence they will fall on. Believe him, or despise him?

EXHAUSTION

There are those in the crowd who are frustrated with the way their lives are going. The family business just failed and the crops will not come, leaving the newborn baby hungry. There are women in the crowd ashamed because they are carrying a baby and they do not know who the father is. There are those who are weighed down by sins committed in secret, hoping to keep them private for fear of what others might think. Fishermen come in from the day's catch with blistered hands, sore backs, empty nets, and empty hearts. Hard and lonely hearts are shattered and broken. This is the crowd Jesus is speaking to.

Yet Jesus is fully aware of the condition of the people. Jesus is not shocked, for he knows their conditions. He knows of their suffering and their distress. With this he utters these words: "Come to me."

I often imagine how it sounded when Jesus said these words. Did he rush through them? Did he yell them out of anger towards the people? Was Jesus stating these words as a question, perhaps uncertain of whether he was capable of fulfilling the needs of the people? I see Jesus pleading to his creation. I see him weeping as he desperately begs for the people to come to him. His eyes are wet with tears, his voice cracks, and his heart aches as he pleads for the people to drink from the only source that will "make you never thirst again."[80] Jesus is not asking. Jesus is not casually offering assistance. Jesus is not hoping the people will respond. Jesus is pleading that the people will take him up on his offer.

Humpty Dumpty had a great fall. We, like Humpty, have all fallen and are in need of assistance. Yet we must not turn to the king's horses and the king's men, hoping they will be able to put us back together, for they will fail. We will never be put back together again if we do not bypass the offerings of this world and go straight to the King. Jesus is pleading for us to allow him to fix us. Jesus is the way, the truth, and the life.[81] Jesus wants to heal us so much that he was willing to have his hands and feet nailed to a cross. While being ridiculed and mocked, beaten and spat upon, and deserted and betrayed, he hung there and pleaded for his creation to come to him to find rest.

Jesus, thank you for your words. Thank you for the invitation to come to you when we are weak and exhausted. Your words are comforting, encouraging, and needed. Father, as we come to you as tired people in need of a Savior, I ask you to fill us with your strength and give us a spirit of perseverance. Thank you for carrying our burdens. Amen.

MILE 23
PERSEVERANCE

"It's at the borders of pain and suffering that the
men are separated from the boys."
—Emil Zatopek

"Patience and perseverance have a magical effect before
which difficulties disappear and obstacles vanish."
—John Quincy Adams

"But those who hope in the Lord will renew their
strength. They will soar on wings like eagles.
They will run and not grow weary, they
will walk and not grow faint."
—Isaiah 40:31

"Therefore, since we are surrounded by such a great
cloud of witnesses, let us throw off everything that
hinders and the sin that so easily entangles us,
and let us run the race with perseverance
the race marked out for us."
—Hebrews 12:1

COUNTDOWNS. EVERYBODY HAS them. It may be a quick glance at the clock in order to figure out how much time is left in your workday. Perhaps it is the number of days between now and the start of spring break. As a kid I loved celebrating countdowns. In elementary school we made paper chains with each link representing one day until that ultimate day. In preparation for Christmas, the artistic among us would alternate red links with green links. Those not in the artistic circle would fight with the tape and simply hope that we had counted the correct number of links (yours truly).

We love countdowns. We love them so much that we now celebrate the day before the actual day. For example, look at Christmas Eve. Lest we forget among all the hype for Christmas Eve, Christmas is the actual holiday. Christmas Eve is the eve of the holiday. Without Christmas, there would be no Christmas Eve. What about New Year's Eve? How many make grand plans for New Year's Day, compared to New Year's Eve? The eve of the day has given us one more thing to count down to.

While countdowns can be entertaining and beneficial, they can also pose a very serious threat. When counting down to a particular day or event, there are only two days that hold any significance—today and the day of the event. All the days in between are assumed to be insignificant. They are mere placeholders or roadblocks between you and your desired destination. However, you will never have a day that is worthless and insignificant. Every day has a reason. Our days here on Earth are limited. We may believe they are endless but the reality is they are not. One day we will breathe our last breath and our earthly existence will end.

How sad it would be to reach that point and realize we had carelessly wished our days away. How unfortunate to look back and realize there were moments we considered worthless and insignificant. There will be seasons of our life we look forward to seeing pass. We will grow tired and weary. When those seasons come upon us, when we reach that mile where everything inside of us is screaming to quit, we must persevere and keep moving forward. It does not matter how slow you are moving. Put one foot in front of the other. Be steadfast. Be Persistent. Persevere.

If required to describe a marathon in one word, I would choose "perseverance." In fact, if only one word could be used to describe running in general, I would still choose perseverance. They seem to be such intimate and accurate representations of each other. Running demands perseverance. There will be moments when you feel like giving up. Days when you simply do not want to run. Moments when your body is screaming at you, yet you continue. You persevere. You keep moving forward despite the obstacles in your way.

Within the context of this book, if I were to write as few words as possible to define and illustrate perseverance I would simply say, "Despite what you feel during Mile 23, you keep going." However, that simplicity does not allow for the opportunity to unpack an amazing portion of Scripture.

Have you ever been reading something only to have one simple word completely sidetrack your train of thought? That happened to me as I was reading Hebrews 12. The author encourages us to have perseverance.

> Therefore since we are surrounded by such a great cloud of witnesses, let us throw off everything that hinders and the sin that so easily entangles. And let us run with perseverance the race marked out for us.[82]

In Hebrews 12, the author conveys that life is going to be tough at times. The Greek word used for "race" is *agona; agona* is where we get our word "agony." The author is describing the race as grueling, difficult, and excruciating. Yet the encouragement comes in that we are to run with perseverance, or in the original Greek, *hupomone,* which translates to cheerful, hopeful endurance and constancy. Though the race is going to be agonizing, we are to run with cheerfulness and hopeful endurance.

There are not many usages of this word throughout the Bible. Upon reading it in Hebrews, I became curious as to where else the word was used. I found a verse that would soon take on a whole new meaning.

> But those who hope in the Lord will renew their strength. They will soar on wings like eagles. They will run and not grow weary, they will walk and not grow faint.[83]

This is perhaps one of the most well-known and commonly quoted passages of Scripture. If you venture into any Christian bookstore, you will find multiple posters, bookmarks, Bible covers, coffee mugs, etc., with this verse imprinted on the object. It is a beautiful verse with an incredible promise. If you see the verse on a poster, do not be surprised if you see it printed on the bottom with a picture of a bald eagle soaring in a blue sky, perhaps with snow-capped mountains in the background.

We love this image because we love the thought of soaring. Eagles can soar over fifteen-thousand feet in the air. Fifteen-thousand feet! That is incredible. Think about the metaphor behind this. We have all been there before. There are moments in life when you feel like you are soaring above the clouds. Thousands of feet in the air, soaring with ease, completely untouchable. The boss just called you into his office to tell you of your promotion. The doctor turns the screen and shows you the image of your child. You attend a weekend retreat with your church and feel as though you have met with God personally and intimately throughout the weekend, giving you the strength to return back to "normal life" full of energy and the determination to change the negative situation in which you have been engulfed.

Sometimes we are soaring. Sometimes we are fifteen-thousand feet in the air meeting intimately with God. Yet sometimes the skies begin to darken; we start to grow weary. Our soar turns into a run. *Agona* creeps in. That new promotion is great, but alongside the benefits come longer hours and working on weekends. The newborn isn't quite so cute at two A.M. when your minimal hours of sleep are interrupted by screams.

PERSEVERANCE

The days of effortlessly soaring are long gone. Your running slows with each step until you can only stagger along, trying not to faint. Your energy is consumed as you walk, crawl, try to hang on, and fight through the pain. A loved one has passed and the empty room seems small compared to the emptiness in your heart. The gossip wheel is spinning and you have no way of clearing your incorrect and undeserved reputation.

The images of this verse—soaring, running walking—epitomize the Christian faith. They accurately describe the different phases we will go through. These three words are a beautiful picture of our journey. Do you know what the most striking part of the picture is? It's Jesus, right beside you through every phase. You may not see him, but he is there. You may not always acknowledge or understand his presence, but it is there. How is he capable of being with you every step of the way? Because the steps you are taking are steps he has already traveled.

Within the first eleven verses of Mark's gospel we get a picture of Jesus soaring. Mark tells the story of Jesus' baptism:

> At that time Jesus came from Nazareth in Galilee and was baptized by John in the Jordan. As Jesus was coming up out of the water, he saw heaven being torn open and the Spirit descending on him like a dove. And a voice came from heaven: "You are my son, whom I love, with you I am well pleased."

Imagine the joy that went through Jesus' heart as he heard those words. God spread the sky and shouted, "THAT'S MY BOY!" What ownership! God the Father was saying, "You are mine!" But he doesn't stop there. His affection gushes as he exclaims, "… whom I love." I wonder if there was a pause between those phrases. Joy and excitement, then a sudden pause, an emotional response as love pours out and affection overwhelms Jesus. And then the acceptance and affirmation, "With you I am well pleased."

Have you ever made your parents so happy with a decision or an action that they were smiling from ear to ear? When you looked at them and saw tears forming in their eyes because they were so pleased to be your parents? We long for that warmth when they put an arm around you and say, "I'm proud of you."

Imagine the creator of the earth having so much pride and joy in you that he spreads the sky and yells for all to hear, "THAT'S MY CHILD ... (pause) I love you. (pause) I'm so proud of you."

Even though he was the Son of God, Jesus was not always soaring. The eleventh chapter of John's gospel gives us a different perspective of Jesus' life. Here we find Jesus busy performing miracles and preaching. During this time he is met with the disheartening news that his good friend Lazarus had passed away. John tells us of the reaction of those who loved Lazarus:

> When Jesus saw her weeping and the Jews who had come along with her also weeping, *he was deeply moved in spirit and troubled.* "Where have you laid him," he asked. "Come and see, Lord," they replied. *Jesus wept.* (Emphasis mine)

After hearing the news of his friend's passing, Jesus wept. The friendship he had enjoyed had come to an end. The soaring that occurred in Mark's gospel had passed and now we find Jesus weeping. He's not soaring, he is running and starting to get weary.

Jesus wept.

If you look at Matthew 26, you will find Jesus in the Garden of Gethsemane. This is not a place of soaring, nor is it a garden where we see our Savior running. It is a garden where Jesus is walking, perhaps even crawling. Jesus is fully aware that he will soon be crucified. He is aware of what is before him. Judas's betrayal. Peter's denial. The disciples scattering upon his arrest. He knows what is coming, and it brings him to his knees.

> My soul is overwhelmed with sorrow, to the point of death ... Father if it is not possible for this cup to be taken away unless I drink, but may your will be done."[84]

Thoughts about coming out of the Jordan water? A faint memory. The weariness from hearing Lazarus is dead? Easy in comparison to this. There is no soaring here. There isn't any

PERSEVERANCE

running. Jesus is having a hard time walking at this point. He is crawling. He is struggling. His heart is overwhelmed.

Through the midst of Jesus' struggle, there are some truths in which we can find peace, encouragement, and security.

First, recognize that Jesus has been there. You have been there. I have been there. There will be times of soaring, times of running, and times of walking and crawling. Take comfort that the path on which you find yourself is not foreign to Jesus. He has been there and he is still there with you. And it is the joy of his heart to be able to be there with you. It is his desire to pour out his love on you. If Jesus was soaring upon coming out of the Jordan and hearing his Father's love for him, surely he is soaring every time you turn to him in a difficult moment and hear him whisper about his love to you.

The second truth is that despite the difficulty, Jesus kept going. In Gethsemane, weary and run down, Jesus very easily could have quit. He could have refused to continue with the plan. Jesus was fully capable of stepping off the course and calling it quits. But he didn't. He kept going.

Sometimes it is difficult not to view Jesus as a little crazy. In the Garden of Gethsemane, Jesus had the opportunity to derail from the plan. He had the chance to avoid what was headed in his direction. He was about to be mocked, flogged, spat upon, stripped of his clothes, forced to wear a mocking thorn of crowns, deserted, and betrayed. That was the easy part. In addition to all that, Jesus took the punishment for all the world's sins—past, present, and future. Sins of the rich, sins of the poor. Sins of those who believe in him and sins of those who curse his name. All sins of all people, all on his shoulders.

What did he do to deserve this punishment? One who has yet to hear of Jesus may be told of all that Jesus went through and come to the conclusion that he must have been an awful person. What he went through was justified because of actions he committed. Their thoughts would lead them to believe Jesus was full of sin himself; full of hatred and destruction. The crazy part is that he was innocent. He was blameless and pure. Having committed no sin, he was perfect. He did not have to continue to the cross, but he chose to. He chose to keep going.

Jesus persevered through the agony because of what would spring from his decision. He was full of eternal hope, knowing his sacrifice would pave the way for him to be the only mediator between man and God. His sights on the future enabled him to persevere and keep going. He had peace and understanding that what he was headed toward was of far greater worth and value compared to the pain he would face. The pain, though far too great for anyone to comprehend, was insignificant compared to the eternal joy made available to the entire world. Jesus chose to persevere.

Mile 23 will not produce pain equivalent to what Jesus felt, but that is OK because you are not the Son of God. Look to Jesus' example and choose to keep going. Regardless of how slow you might be running, keep going. Without any care as to what you may look like, keep going. Pushing aside the pain of how you feel, keep going. At this point in the race do not be afraid to start looking toward the finish line. You are almost there. Allow yourself to think about the feeling that will overcome your body as you cross the finish line. The satisfaction and feelings of accomplishment. Look forward, hopeful and joyful for what awaits you. Perhaps it will be family or friends. Maybe it will be a cold beverage, and most important, the finish line. Anticipate what is yet to come, and keep going until you are there.

When the agonies of life come our way, perseverance is needed. The reason behind the agony could be as plentiful as minutes in a day. Jesus has been there, and it is the joy of his heart to be there with you now. While running and growing weary, or walking and growing faint, it is hard to keep your head above the water. In those moments may you be strengthened, knowing that Jesus will never leave you nor forsake you. May you be encouraged, knowing that Jesus will be with you even to the end of the age. Find the strength to keep going. Don't give up. Don't quit. Persevere.

PERSEVERANCE

Jesus, thank you for showing us the way. Thank you for being an example for us to follow. It is encouraging to know that you have experienced the troubles of this life and the different phases we will go through. Jesus, you have been there, and you have kept going. Please give us the perseverance to keep going. Father, I want to pray specifically for those who might be going through hard times. You understand the groans of their hearts. You hear their cries and you see their tears. Father, comfort them. Provide for them. Fill them with your peace and your joy. Jesus, the troubles of this world are difficult but you promised that you would never leave us. We cling to that promise now. And Lord, as crazy as it may sound, we thank you for these trials, knowing they will help shape us more into your image, even if we cannot see it or understand it here on this earth. Father, you are good. You are real. Thank you, Father. Amen.

MILE 24
GRATITUDE

"Be thankful for your trials. If you're being tested, you're being perfected, which means you have a divine purpose and reason to rejoice."
—Unknown

"Gratitude changes the pangs of memory into a tranquil joy."
—Dietrich Bonhoeffer

"O come, let us sing unto the LORD; let us make a joyful noise to the rock of our salvation. Let us come before his presence with thanksgiving, and make a joyful noise unto him with psalms."
—Psalm 95:1

"One of them, when he saw he was healed, came back, praising God in a loud voice."
—Luke 17:15

I WAS WELL into my twenties before I knew the man responsible for the holiday that is the American Thanksgiving. Having never thought much about Thanksgiving's origin, I always assumed it started with the Pilgrims and Indians (or "Native Americans"—I'm not sure what is more politically correct at the moment) and continued on from the "first Thanksgiving" consistently to the most recent Thanksgiving we celebrated. Years ago, had you asked me to name the "Father of Thanksgiving," I probably would have answered Squanto or maybe John Smith. Maybe I'm just ignorant and cannot fully remember all I was taught in my early years of education.

A few years ago I was invited to a Thanksgiving party with friends, and those attending were encouraged to dress up as "typical" Thanksgiving characters. Along with a co-worker I went dressed as a classy pilgrim, complete with a top hat made out of cardboard and black soccer socks for leggings. There were a few Indians in attendance as well as a few other pilgrims. But the one person I was not expecting was Abraham Lincoln. In fact, when I saw my friend dressed in a nice suit, I was pretty confused as to whom he was supposed to be. My friend decided to keep his identity secret until we all sat down at the table. Then in a very entertaining way he revealed who he was and informed everyone that Abraham Lincoln was the President who helped establish Thanksgiving as a national holiday in the United States.

While there is some debate as to the exact history of Thanksgiving, there is one generally well-received timeline. The first Thanksgiving was celebrated in 1621 with, as we all know, the Pilgrims and Indians. Despite what most assume, including me until I did a little more searching, these two groups did not hold a similar party the following year. In fact, it was quite a few years before the Pilgrims celebrated again.

The second celebration may or may not have included the Indians, as history does not make that clear. Close to a hundred years passed before this holiday was widely observed for the second time in 1777. The reason for this celebration was not directly connected to the original celebration as much as it was a time to celebrate

GRATITUDE

the victory over the British in the American Revolution. Shortly thereafter, President George Washington proclaimed Thanksgiving a national day, which was a few years later opposed by President Thomas Jefferson. This left the day generally uncelebrated until 1863 when President Abraham Lincoln established Thanksgiving as a national holiday on the last Thursday of November. President Franklin Roosevelt later tinkered with the date (now it is the fourth Thursday of November), but it was Abraham Lincoln who generally gets credit for Thanksgiving as a national holiday.

Thanksgiving is one of those holidays that brings out great traditions. Who gets to fight for the wishbone, who makes the gravy, when you watch the football games—all aspects of the day that will differ with each family. While traditions may vary, there is one that many people hold in common: sharing with others at least one thing for which they are thankful.

Am I the only one who finds it a bit odd, and sad, that we can be dependent on a holiday to encourage us to have "a time of thankfulness"? Does anyone else feel a little shallow when you are sitting at the table listening to others share their thankful thoughts and all you can come up with is a stereotypical answer? Outside the week of Thanksgiving, how often do we stop and think about things we are thankful for?

Within Luke's Gospel we are introduced to a character whose name is not revealed. Regardless of why his name is never mentioned, the Holy Spirit knew we would need to hear this man's story. The story indicates that ten men were suffering with leprosy when they came across Jesus' path. Aware of the cultural regulations of the day, the men kept their distance and cried out to Jesus. Upon hearing them, Jesus gave them instructions and as they followed his words they were healed.

In conversations surrounding the church crowd today, it is not uncommon to hear the phrase, "I feel so distant from God right now." There are times when it seems as though our prayers are only heard by the walls around us. Circumstances, whether in or out of our control, make us feel as if God is far away. I wonder what the distance between these ten lepers and Jesus was. I also wonder how loud they had to yell in order to be heard. How long had they been outside the city gates waiting for Jesus? How many nights had they slept outside the gates lonely and disheartened?

There may be times when you feel distant from God. He seems far off and you cannot seem to connect with him. You cannot feel his comfort or his healing hand. But in reading Luke 17 we see that Jesus heard these lepers. He heard their cries. Similarly, he hears your cries. He knows your pain and he hears your heart's groans. I don't know why God answers some prayers and not others. I do not understand why he moves when he does. But I trust him. I have found him faithful and true. If you find yourself crying out in the distance, be comforted and encouraged to know that Jesus hears you.

As Jesus hears the cries of the lepers, he sends them off and heals them. All ten take off running as they follow his instructions. After being healed of their leprosy, nine keep running while one stops and heads back to where he came from. Did the other nine discourage him from turning around? Were they too selfish to even notice that he was gone? Did the one who turned around announce where he was going or did he keep his agenda hidden out of fear of what the others would say or think? We are given no details. We only know he found his way back to Jesus.

Luke uses great imagery as we read about this character's return to Jesus. He *threw* himself at Jesus' feet.[85] Just a few verses prior to this he was yelling in the distance, unable and too afraid to get close. Now distance is not an issue. The praise and thanks he has for Jesus is so overwhelming that he throws himself at Jesus' feet. Within this description Luke also includes one aspect to the story that should be noted—the man was a Samaritan. Within the culture it was taboo for Gentiles and Samaritans to interact. Diseases aside and cultural standards disregarded, this man had his life changed by Jesus and he was full of gratitude.

Which character best represents you in this story? Are you one of the nine who rarely thinks to come back and thank Jesus? Or are you the one who throws himself at Jesus' feet with a thankful heart? We are taught by our parents to say "please" and "thank you." We

GRATITUDE

have a national holiday to celebrate that for which we are thankful. Yet does our gratitude really permeate all we do?

As you run through Mile 24, allow yourself to think about all you are grateful for. Whether directly related to running or not, may these steps be marked with gratitude. There are times throughout life when circumstances fog our vision and prevent us from seeing anything over which we can be thankful. Set forth below are a few different aspects of running for which I am thankful.

Comfort runs. In New Hampshire there is one trail I have run too many times to count. I have run it so many times that I literally have a favorite step that I am forced to take every time because of the bend of the trail and the trees overhead. On difficult days, that trail was a close friend, always willing to listen to me rant and rave whether through words or the huffing and puffing of my breathing. Comfort runs are reliable and a great boost, just like Grandma's snickerdoodles and apple cider.

Training partners. Those both near and far. Those who encourage, inspire, and motivate. They are there to bring out the best in you and they desire to see you grow. They will call you out when you are giving less than your best, and they will call you when you are struggling.

Hills. OK, this sounds crazy. Why would anyone be grateful for steep inclines that make your legs burn and ache? What is good about your heart feeling like it is about to jump out of your chest, and realizing you have only made it ten feet? Hills are hard, but hills are good. They make you stronger physically, mentally, and emotionally. Plus you often are rewarded with a beautiful view at the top.

Freedom. Time is a commodity in short supply. There are constantly people or things vying for our attention, energy, and time. When you are on that trail, you are free. You can go where you want to go. You determine the speed at which you want to run.

Days off. Rest. What a beautiful thing. Something we all need. A break from running would not be as refreshing if you did not run in the first place. Days off are opportunities for your body to recover and relax. They are an opportunity for your body to rebuild the muscle that was torn down from previous exercises.

Running. This is something that may be so simple and basic that it gets overlooked. While running, be thankful for the fact that you are running! Regardless of size, speed, endurance, or experience, you are out there running. The fact that you can run, that you are physically capable of lacing up your shoes and feeling the breeze hit your face, is itself something for which to be grateful.

There are certainly more aspects that could be added to the list. What is provided is a small sample that will hopefully allow you to come up with your own list of reasons to be grateful for running. I encourage you, whether in the space provided below or elsewhere, to write down a few different things you are grateful for. Perhaps taking a moment to focus on the positive will enable you to stop dwelling on the negative.

Father, we come before you with grateful hearts. You have given us so much. Despite all the wickedness in our hearts, you chose to love us. Even though we live in ways that oppose your holiness, you sent your Son to die for us. Father, we are thankful for your love. We are thankful for your Son and for his sacrifice. May this gratitude overwhelm our hearts and transform the way in which we live. Amen.

MILE 25
RESOLVE

"There is no chance, no destiny, no fate that can
circumvent or hinder or control the firm
resolve of a determined soul."
—Ella Wheeler Wilcox

"Obstacles cannot crush me. Every obstacle yields to
stern resolve. He who is fixed to a star does
not change his mind."
—Leonardo da Vinci

"I was only the servant of my country and had I,
at any moment, failed to express her unflinching
resolve to fight and conquer, I should at once
have been rightly cast aside."
—Winston Churchill

"Seven days from now I [God] will send rain on the earth
for forty days and forty nights, and I will wipe from the
face of the earth every living creature I have made."
—Genesis 7:4

YOU ANXIOUSLY SIT in front of the computer, full of uncertainty, fear, and excitement. Your credit card is sitting next to the mouse. You have done your homework and all the research. The weekend of the marathon is promising to be ideal—you have a place to stay, easy transportation for race day, and other logistics. Even though you have yet to register, you are already training. As you stare at the computer screen, you realize if you click "register" there is no turning back.

Up to this point you have talked about running a marathon but have not committed to one. Whether you realize it or not, there is some freedom in that. You can talk to family and friends about the intention you have of running and receive all of their jaw-dropping awe and enthusiasm without being completely locked in. So you sit and stare at the computer screen, internally debating if this decision is one you are absolutely certain about. Finally you grab the mouse and with a single click, you are officially registered. Now you must exhibit what you already possess—resolve; the mental and emotional strength to reach a definitive decision despite difficulty, adversity, and danger.

Perhaps you have never found yourself in the situation described above, but I imagine the majority of us at one point were smacked across the face with the question, "What in the world did I sign myself up for?" Those moments of difficulty and adversity open the floodgates of doubt and uncertainty. Those moments are when you must rely on the resolve within you. The determination and drive that led you to click "register" will lead you to the race and through the race.

As you run through Mile 25, one in which a resolved spirit is vital, I want to encourage you with two separate thoughts; one pertaining to your decision to run and the second concerning those times in which things do not go according to plan.

At this point in the race you are most likely tired. Even elite marathoners admit that fatigue can creep in and crush the body and mind. Regardless of age, speed, and skill, one thing binds everyone together—we all made the decision to run. As John Bingham stated, "If you run, you are a runner. It does not matter how fast or how

RESOLVE

far. It does not matter if today is your first day or if you've been running for twenty years. There is no test to pass, no license to earn, no membership card to get. You just run." So regardless of ability, everyone at Mile 25 is a runner. And all of those runners contain the resolve that helped them decide to run a marathon. Aware of the difficulty and adversity that lay ahead, you decided to run. At this point you must return to that resolve and allow it to propel you forward. Have the determination to take each step that will soon carry you across the finish line.

Sometimes the steps throughout this mile can bring disappointment. At this juncture, some runners may find themselves in a position they were hoping to avoid. In looking back at my third marathon, I have to throw myself in this category. Mile 25 brought significant pain, physically, mentally, and emotionally. Throughout this mile I knew I would cross the finish line in a time slower than my intended goal. I had not planned on cramping. I had not anticipated the heat. I had not anticipated performing so poorly. Things were not going according to the plan I had drawn up. There were times in which I was convinced I had taken my final step. I had one eye on the road and the other on the sideline, looking for a place I could easily transform from participant to observer. Despite the strong wishes of my cramping calf muscles and quads, I was determined to take each step necessary to cross the finish line.

Things will not always go according to plan. But in those moments, may you be reminded of what you have accomplished to this point and may you be filled with resolve.

In doing some research for this chapter I came across a number of stories about individuals who possessed and exhibited great amounts of resolve. I share their stories here with the hope of providing encouragement and inspiration.

Johnny Fulton was run over by a car at the age of three. He suffered crushed hips, broken ribs, a fractured skull, and compound fractures in his legs. It did not look as if he would live. But he would not give up. In fact, he later ran the half-mile in less than two minutes.

Walt Davis was totally paralyzed by polio when he was nine years old, but he did not give up. He became the Olympic high jump champion in 1952.

Shelly Mann was paralyzed by polio when she was five years old. She eventually claimed eight different swimming records for the USA and won a gold medal at the 1956 Olympics in Melbourne, Australia.

In 1938, Karoly Takacs, a member of Hungary's world-champion pistol shooting team and a sergeant in the army, lost his right hand when a grenade he was holding exploded. He didn't let it deter him. He learned to shoot left-handed and won gold medals in the 1948 and 1952 Olympics.

Lou Gehrig was such a clumsy ball player that the boys in his neighborhood would not let him play on their team. But he was committed. Eventually, his name was entered into baseball's Hall of Fame.

Woodrow Wilson could not read until he was ten years old. But he was determined. He became the twenty-eighth President of the United States.

The Bible has numerous accounts of how God's people displayed resolve. One such man was Noah. Noah was a righteous and blameless man in a world full of wickedness. Despite the mocking cries and voices of doubt from those around him, Noah listened to God's calling and built an ark, saving his family and establishing a new covenant with God.

Noah made a decision, and despite all the uncertainty and harassment that followed, he continued on his path, knowing it was the one that God had led him to. If you think people give you bizarre looks and comments when they hear that you are running a marathon, think of what Noah faced. For starters, he was an old man. By the time the first rain drop fell, Noah was six hundred years old. Yet despite his age he was building an enormous boat, a boat bigger than any had seen or imagined. Add to this his mandate to collect all of the animals on the earth. And that Noah entered the ark and remained there for seven days without a drop of rain.

RESOLVE

Noah's deciding to stay inside the ark during that seven-day stretch without any rain illustrates his resolve.

During those seven days Noah stood up for what he believed. There is no account of what his neighbors said to him or of Noah's thoughts during this time. Therefore, we are forced to speculate a little about the way things played out.

The text tells us that the men and women of that time were full of evil in everything they did. "Every inclination of the thoughts of his [all men and women] heart was *only evil all the time*."[86] Again with a bit of speculating I believe the men and women encamped around Noah and heckled him. They mocked him, his crazy boat, and his bizarre thoughts of rain. Despite the insults, Noah decided to stand up for what he believed and whom he believed in.

Additionally, Noah was unwilling to waver in his decision to follow God. I imagine Noah envisioned bringing his family and all the animals into the ark and following the loud thud from the door closing, the first boom of thunder would crackle. Not so much. Sometimes God's timing does not match up with our own. Noah entered the ark and sat there, one day, two days, three days, and beyond. The mocking cries of the passers-by only increased as each day passed. If Noah's neighbors were jeering him while he was building the boat, one can only imagine what the chants were while Noah was inside the boat for a few days and not a single drop of rain had yet to fall. I wonder if Noah crawled to the bottom of the ark, fell to his knees, and cried the prayer so many of us have cried, "God, where are you? Have you forgotten about me? Have you brought me to this place to abandon me now?"

As the story unfolds, we continue to see Noah's resolve. Despite things not going according to Noah's timeline, he did not give up. There was certainly difficulty, perhaps frustration, and sprinkles of confusion. Despite this, Noah made the decision to follow God, and he would not go back on that decision.

I stop and look at Noah's resolve and ask myself, "How did he remain true to his decision? Why did he continue to have faith?" I can find no other answer than these two words: God's faithfulness.

God had proven himself faithful in the past and Noah relied on this in his moments of difficulty. Two instances that exemplify this point: all of the animals that came to Noah and the fact that God shut him in the ark.

Noah did not go out recruiting all of the animals; they came to him. Noah was given the task of making sure all the animals were in the ark, a task that seems quite difficult, perhaps almost as difficult as building an ark. I wonder if there were days when Noah was having difficulty, days when his neighbors were jeering him and his patience was running low. Days when doubt started to creep in and Noah wondered what he was really doing. Just at the moment when Noah put down his hammer and thought about walking away, he witnessed a couple of elephants walking his way. The elephants came and lifted his spirits. They brought reassurance and boosted his energy. When Noah was in the ark on day five he may have been a bit discouraged. But during those moments he heard the elephants and he was reminded of how God brought them to him at just the right time once before. He knew that God would be faithful again.

In addition to the animals, God provided a lasting memory for Noah to recall when he shut the door. It does not appear that Noah played any part in closing the door. In Genesis 7:16 we read, "… then the Lord shut him in." Imagine the scene; the animals have just gotten settled in their bunks, Noah's family is on board, and their neighbors are outside pointing at the sun and laughing at Noah, when all of a sudden the door starts to close. No human is within fifteen feet of the door, yet it is moving. The door is too big to be closed by the wind, so onlookers scratch their heads. They are witnessing a miracle as they are watching the hand of God moving. While Noah's family is being shut in, the neighbors are being shut up and shut out. At the same time, Noah is taking note of yet another time in which God showed up and proved himself faithful.

God is faithful. He has shown up before and he will do so again. It may not necessarily look exactly how we want, or how we imagine, but this does not mean he is unfaithful. In the final steps

RESOLVE

of Mile 25, may you run with resolve. Continue to push forward. You are about to begin the joyous final mile of the race.

Father, thank you for your faithfulness. Thank you for showing up. We acknowledge that there are times when you don't show up in the way we would like. However, even in those times may we find rest and peace in your faithfulness and in your character. I thank you for Mile 25 and all it has to teach us. May we become better servants as a result of what we have learned. Amen.

MILE 26
JOY

"Running! If there's any activity happier, more exhilarating, more nourishing to the imagination, I can't think of what it might be. In running the mind flees with the body, the mysterious efflorescence of language seems to pulse in the brain, in rhythm with our feet and the swinging of our arms."
—Joyce Carol Oates

"I am the gate; whoever enters through me will be saved. He will come in and go out and find pasture. The thief comes only to steal and kill and destroy; I have come that they may have life, and have it to the full."
—John 10:10

RUNNING THROUGH LIFE

*F*OR MANY THERE are many uncertainties that occur immediately after college graduation. Among the wide depth of uncertainty, however, there is a constant occurrence: weddings. In the weeks and months that follow college, many graduates initiate this new part of their life with marriage. The weekdays are busy with moving out, job interviews, and apartment shopping while the weekends are spent at weddings. Unfortunately, in moving to Germany following my graduation from college, it was impossible for me to attend every wedding that I was invited to. I desperately tried to be present at many of them, but logistically I only could attend a few. Those were difficult days for me. Knowing I was in Germany thousands of miles away while my close friends were gathering to celebrate new chapters in life was disheartening. I am thankful my friends showed me grace and understanding when I could not attend, but it was never easy for me to be absent.

When I was able to attend a wedding, it was always a beautiful and joyous occasion. I cannot remember how or when it started, but after attending a few different weddings I began to change where I fixed my gaze as the wedding began. Rather than turn and watch the doors open and witness the bride walk through, I began to keep my eyes focused on the groom. I would wait and watch him. Without fail, by watching the expression of the groom's face, I would know the precise moment the doors flung open behind me.

To date there is one wedding where this is most memorable for me. We were gathered in Virginia in the middle of the summer for an outdoor wedding. I had known the groom for close to six years at the time of his wedding and was privileged to be a groomsman. He is an incredible man, and a great friend, and also a very talented runner. As the groomsmen took their places up front, I purposely moved slightly out of line in order to ensure that I had a view of the groom. The procession of bridesmaids started and I could see that he was getting excited and antsy. He was slightly fidgety and perhaps a little nervous (and who could blame him—thirty minutes prior to the start of the wedding we realized we had forgotten his wedding ring back at the hotel, which was thirty-five minutes away). The final bridesmaid made her way down the aisle. Everyone stood and turned. For a moment there was complete silence. Virtually every eye was fixed on where the bride would enter, but I was looking at the groom. The music started, the doors opened, and I was moved to tears as I gazed at my friend. He had seen his bride and his face was radiant. He was beaming. His face spoke deeply of the love, passion, excitement, and joy he had for his bride. He was emotional and started to cry a little as well (which is what set me off). It was a blessing and touching for me to be able to see my close friend so full of joy. Soon the bride and groom met each other and joined hands. She noticed his tears and said something to make him laugh and ease his nerves. Simply put, it was beautiful. Their joy was moving, contagious, and obvious.

The concept of joy is what I will discuss as we move toward the finish line in this, the final portion of the marathon. Throughout this mile, allow yourself to sit back (figuratively speaking, of course) and enjoy it. The previous few miles were marked by perseverance, tenacity, endurance, exhaustion, etc. Not so with Mile 26. This is the mile of joy; the mile of celebration.

Throughout Mile 26 I encourage you to take joy and satisfaction in what you have accomplished. Not only have you accomplished much during the previous twenty-five miles, you have achieved much during the many miles you logged while training for the race. In previous chapters we looked at the tedious nature of training and the toll it can take on your mind and body. Similar to "hitting the wall" during the actual race, you may have also hit a wall in your training. Despite the weeks of training, the hills, the mountaintops, the setbacks, and the victories, you fought your way to the start line. Now you find yourself within a mile of the finish line. Take joy in that.

There are those who will find joy during this mile (actually, it's the final 1.2 miles, but at this point, the extra .2 is merely frosting on the cake) as they accomplish something they once deemed impossible. Many who cross the finish line will do so after hearing words of doubt from those around them, such as "You're crazy for attempting that. You'll never finish." As you take those final steps, you are doing it. You are about to reach the finish line. Be proud of yourself, be happy with your performance. Do not worry about what the time on the clock says, do not be discouraged or intimidated; rather, be full of joy. Congratulations on doing what once seemed impossible.

Listen to the noise and energy emanating from the crowd. Mile 7 was epitomized by loneliness; such is not the case during this final stretch. I recall the twenty-sixth mile from my race in Switzerland with great fondness. I was still a ways away, yet I could hear the music loud and clear. The roar from the crowd was continually increasing as the number of people lining the course seemed to be equally escalating. It is as if the people at this point are not only cheering for you; they are cheering with you. They have probably never seen you before and likely will never see you again, yet for the brief moments as you pass they cheer as if you are their best friend. You should not be surprised if you receive multiple high-fives from those lining the streets. This mile is filled with joy. Enjoy the music, the cheers, and the celebration.

There is an image for you to enjoy during the last mile, and that is of a victory lap. This mile is your victory lap. With the music loud, and the fans louder, you have a chance to enjoy your final steps of the race. You now have more than twenty-five miles behind you, plus all of your training miles. You worked hard for those miles and gave everything you had. While this mile will definitely be no different in that respect, it will feel unique in that this mile is your victory lap. You have earned it. You deserve it. Enjoy!

As the last words of this book are written, I leave you with one final word of encouragement: Be men and women of joy. I realize that is easier said than done, but I am praying that Jesus' words that come to us through the Gospel of John prove as the mantra and reality check we may be in need of.

All Christians should be joyous. But there is a difference between joy and happiness. All Christians will not always be happy, and that is formidable. There are books dedicated entirely to this topic. Happiness is circumstantial while joy is eternal. Our happiness can and will fluctuate, and this is often due to the circumstances we find ourselves in. Our joy should not waver, however, as it is eternal and founded in the knowledge that our sins have been paid for by the blood of Jesus Christ.

Throughout life there will be moments that are less than happy, but they can still be filled with joy. Only weeks prior to my high school graduation, my younger sister was involved in a life-threatening and life-changing car accident. So many moments throughout that trial are vivid in my mind as if they happened yesterday. I can still recite the words of the first phone call we received informing us of the accident, and the drive that ensued to be by my sister's side. Walking into the hospital where she was momentarily held prior to being air lifted to a larger hospital was such a blur as there were so many unknowns and so many emotions, yet I could repeat my mom's exact movements and words as we got a brief sight of my sister as she was being taken to the helicopter that would fly her down to Boston.

The hours and days that followed were filled with little sleep and many doctors using terminology I did not understand. There were many unknowns. If one were to ask the doctor, "Is she going to make it?" the reply would have been, "We are going to do all we can but we are not sure." For the second time in my life I was forced into a role of mere observer as one of my family members was fighting for life. Four years prior to this when I went to bed at night I did not know whether I would wake up and find my dad alive. Now I was trying to fall asleep as my little sister was fighting for her life, unaware if I would ever hear her voice again.

It may sound crazy, in fact I am certain it does, but even in those dark hours while in the Intensive Care Unit at Massachusetts General Hospital, as doctors were monitoring the amount of swelling and bleeding in my sister's brain and as she was hooked up to a tube that helped her to breathe since her punctured lung was incapable of doing so on its own, there was joy. As my mom, dad, and brother gathered by her bedside, we were joyful. Our happiness was gone the moment we received that first phone call, but at that moment we all witnessed how fleeting and miniscule our happiness was in comparison to our joy.

Joy in the midst of tragedy? Peace in a hospital room filled with unknowns? How is that possible? It comes from a God who became man. It is possible because the Creator came to his creation to accomplish what we could not accomplish on our own. The impossible is possible since the perfect one took the punishment and paid the price for the imperfect. He who knew no sin became the sacrifice. He never sinned yet suffered as if he did. He brought hope to the hopeless. Rest to the weary. Joy to the saddened.

In John's Gospel he records Jesus describing himself as the Good Shepherd. The Shepherd who will lay down his life for his sheep. A Shepherd who knows his sheep and they know him and his voice. In this account Jesus states, "The thief comes only to steal and kill and destroy; I have come that they may have life, and have it to the full."[87] We can find peace in a world of unrest and joy in the middle of tragedy.

Our joy is eternally based. Jesus states that he came so that we may have life to the full. Other translations refer to this as abundant life, life in all its fullness. My favorite translation is "I have come that they may have life, the real kind of life." We were not made for this earth. We were made for eternity and we were made for heaven. Life on Earth is not all there is. When one comes to faith in Jesus and is certain of where he or she will spend eternity, that is great cause for joy, a joy that cannot be dampened or destroyed by the things of this world.

James in his book encourages us to consider it pure joy when we face many different trials.[88] This brings me great encouragement. It reminds us that we will face trials. James provides a bit of foreshadowing and gives us a heads-up that difficulties will come our way. However, he encourages us with the assurance that these trials, though difficult, will shape us more into the image of Jesus Christ. Trials can also serve as a reminder that we will spend eternity in a place where suffering does not exist. What joy that instills in our hearts!

I urge you to embrace the joy that we have in Jesus Christ. We will not all live lives full of bliss, free from headaches and heartaches. Turn on the nightly news and you will quickly see the dark world in which we live. Yet there is a light within us, a light that has defeated the darkness. While trials may come and kidnap your happiness, they cannot capture your joy.

For those who may be going through trials, may you be encouraged and reminded of the joy you have from Jesus. May those who witness you in the hospital room, at the funeral home, or in the cancer hospice recognize that you are different from the others they have seen. May your doctor hear peace in your voice as you face your trial knowing that, regardless of the outcome, your eternity is going to be spent with Jesus.

While going through the trial of my sister's accident, I clung to the lyrics of the song "None But Jesus" by Hillsong United. The title in itself proved to be a great reminder of where my joy is rooted. Those days were not fun. They were not easy. But, they were filled with joy because of Jesus.

> There is no one else for me
> None but Jesus
> Crucified to set me free
> Now I live to bring him praise.
> In the chaos, in confusion
> I know You're sovereign still
> In the moment of my weakness
> You give me grace to do your will.

Those moments, wondering whether I would ever hear my sister's voice again, were extremely difficult for me. While I typed these words, my sister was energetically dancing around me, singing and talking (even though no one was listening). The road continues to have bumps and bruises, but her presence is a daily reminder of God's goodness, and of the joy that can only be found through him.

It is my prayer that you are able to finish the marathon with joy. May your victory lap be pleasant, fun, and enjoyable.

I am going to end where we started this chapter, at a wedding. In Virginia I was staring at the groom and I saw a face that was overcome with emotion. He was filled with joy as his bride appeared and started walking toward him. His body shook, his lips quivered, and tears fell from his eyes.

Jesus has told us that we are his bride. He has come to be our groom and to usher us into eternity. Our sins have created a dark spot that were washed away by his blood. We will appear white as snow in his presence and as his bride.

I cannot wait to see the joy on the groom's face on that day.

Father, thank you for the joy we have in you. This world will bring us many different trials that will darken our days, yet you have overcome the darkness. You are the light of the world. You have come to set us free and allow us to live a life of abundance, the real kind of life, an eternity spent with you. Thank you. Thank you for carrying us through these 26.2 miles. I pray they were miles of learning and growth ... and joy. Lord, you are good. We need none but you. Amen.

ENDNOTES

1. 1 Sam. 17
2. Num. 14
3. Est. 4
4. Acts 1
5. Titus 2:7-8
6. Dan. 6:26-27
7. 2 Tim. 1:7
8. Heb. 12:1
9. Gen. 29
10. Rom. 1:8-10
11. 1 Cor. 1:4
12. 1 Cor. 13:4
13. 1 Peter 2:9a
14. 1 Peter 2:9b
15. 1 Peter 2:12
16. 1 Peter 4:3-4
17. Gen. 2
18. 1 Thess. 4:18
19. Prov. 27:17
20. Heb. 10:24
21. 2 Tim. 4:2

22. Num. 27:16-17
23. 1 Sam. 18:1-4
24. Dan. 3
25. Acts 4:36
26. Heb. 2:14-18
27. Heb. 4:14-16
28. 2 Cor. 1:3-4
29. Luke 6:12; Luke 22:39-46
30. John 15:5-7
31. Neh. 4:17
32. *Max Lucado Daily: You're Pre-Packed.* January 9, 2012
33. 1 Cor. 9:22b
34. Deut. 31:7
35. Ps. 23:1
36. Neh. 2:8
37. Isa. 41:10
38. Est. 4:16
39. Est. 3:8-9
40. Est. 4:16a
41. Est. 4:16
42. John 4
43. Rom. 8:28
44. Paraphrase of 1 Kings 17:1
45. 1 Kings 17:3-4
46. Paraphrase of 1 Kings 17:18
47. 1 Kings 18:29
48. 1 Kings 18:38
49. 1 Kings 18:46, emphasis added
50. Gen. 39
51. Gen. 40:6
52. Gen. 41:38
53. Gen. 41:38-40
54. Gen. 50:19-21
55. Rom. 5:8
56. John 4:19

ENDNOTES

57. 2:03:59 was run at the Boston Marathon in 2011, but that time is not considered eligible to be counted in world records due to slope changes throughout the course.
58. Taken from my personal running journal on July 7, 2010.
59. Taken from my personal running journal on August 15, 2010.
60. Dan. 3:16
61. Dan. 3:28
62. Gen. 22:5
63. Mark 7:6
64. Phil. 3:20
65. 2 Tim. 4:7-8
66. Rev. 3:20
67. Rom. 3:23
68. Rom. 5:8
69. John 14:6
70. John 3:16
71. Ex. 5:22
72. Ex. 6:20, emphasis added
73. Luke 8:42-48
74. Luke 8:42
75. Heb. 12:2
76. Josh. 1:5
77. Matt. 28:2-3
78. Matt. 11:28
79. Matt. 11:29
80. Rev. 7:16
81. John 14:6
82. Heb. 12:1-2
83. Isa. 40:31
84. Matt. 26:38-39
85. Luke 17:16
86. Gen. 6:5, emphasis added
87. John 10:10
88. James 1:2

WinePressPublishing
Great Books, Defined.

To order additional copies of this book call:
1-877-421-READ (7323)
or please visit our website at
www.WinePressbooks.com

If you enjoyed this quality custom-published book, drop by our website for more books and information.

www.winepresspublishing.com

"Your partner in custom publishing."